Mathematics Key Stage 3 Tests

Ewart Smith

Stanley Thornes (Publishers) Ltd

First published 1997 by

Stanley Thornes (Publishers) Ltd,
Ellenborough House,
Wellington Street,
CHELTENHAM
GL50 1YW

A catalogue record of this book is available from the British Library.

ISBN 0 7487 3166 0

97 98 99 00 01 / 10 9 8 7 6 5 4 3 2 1

Illustrated by Linda Jeffrey, Mike Ing
Typeset by Tech Set Ltd
Printed and bound in Great Britain

Contents

Preface

This book consists of two practice tests for Key Stage 3 mathematics. Each test has two papers. Every paper contains 30 questions which are grouped according to level, and range from level 3 to level 8. The questions belonging to each group are clearly marked so that, for example, a potential candidate for Tier 4–6 would attempt questions 7 to 21. Some questions test work in more than one level. A calculator is not allowed for Paper 1 but is allowed for Paper 2.

While the layout of the questions is similar to that used in the May tests it is not intended that the tests in this book are timed accurately. More questions are included than is the case for an actual test. This will enable the teacher to select what is considered most beneficial for his/her immediate needs within the class time available. The book is not a workbook; consequently some material will need to be copied into the pupil's exercise book before it can be used. Apart from a pen, pencil, rubber and ruler, the pupil may require an angle measurer or protractor, tracing paper or a mirror, and a pair of compasses. Where there is a need for any of this equipment there is a note at the beginning of the question. The allocation of marks is left to the discretion of the teacher.

Mental test material is available to teachers, along with the answers, in a separate free supplement.

It is hoped that by using this book pupils and teachers will be better prepared for these important tests.

Ewart Smith 1997

TEST 1 Paper 1

Do not use a calculator for this test.

Level 3 • Questions 1 to 6

1. Here are some packets of screws.

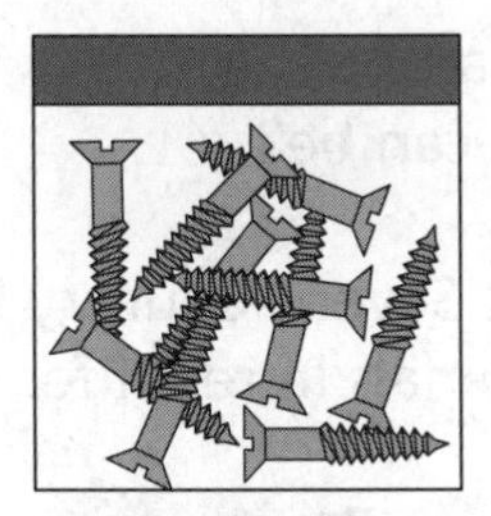

10 countersink screws

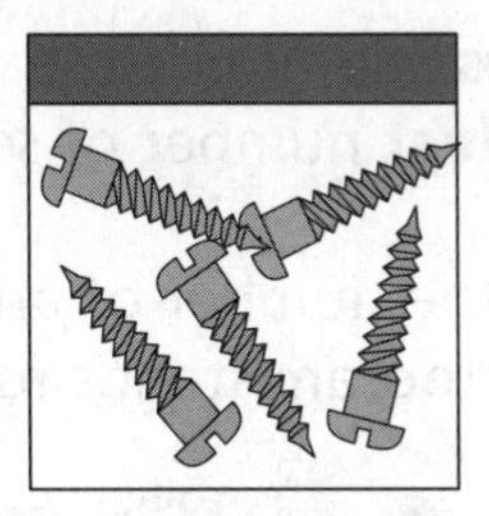

5 cheese-headed screws

2 round-headed screws

a Clive bought **8** packets of **cheese-headed** screws. How many screws did he buy?

b Ed bought **7** packets of **countersink** screws
and **4** packets of **round-headed** screws.
How many screws did he buy?

c Betty bought **exactly 12** screws. They were all the same kind. What kind of screws did she buy?

d Meg bought **exactly 25** screws.
They were all the same kind.
What kind of screws did Meg buy?

e Ross wants **exactly 60** screws. They must all be the **same kind**.
Copy these statements and fill in the blanks.

Ross could buy 6 packets of .... screws

or .... packets of rounded-headed screws

or .... packets of .... screws.

2a The number on the register at St John's School is **1073**. What is this correct to the nearest **hundred**?

b The school has **63** staff. What is this to the nearest **ten**?

c The school cost **£1 793 824** to build. What is this correct to the nearest **thousand** pounds?

d The number of seats that can be laid out in the school hall is **800**, correct to the nearest **hundred**.

(i) What is the **largest** number of seats this can be?
(ii) What is the **smallest** number of seats this can be?

3. The pictogram shows the number of animals at Severn Country Park. **Each** animal in the pictogram stands for **10** animals in real life.

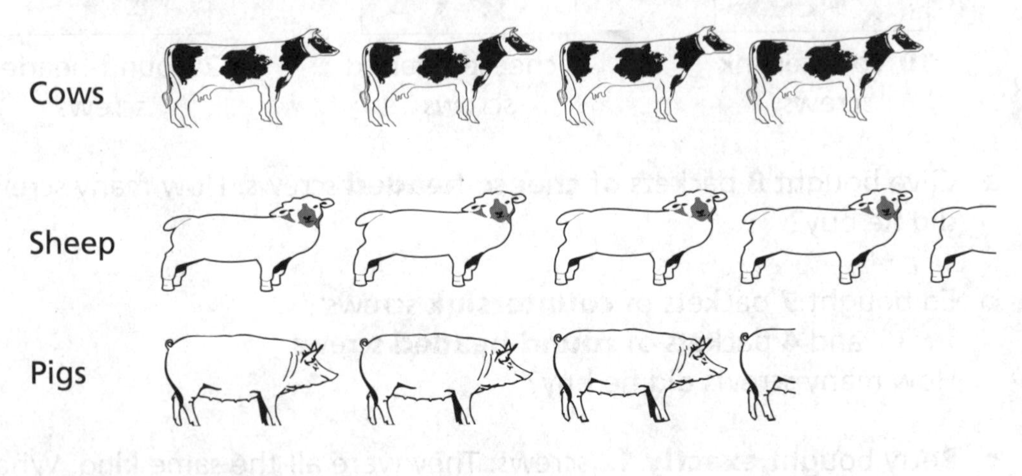

a How many **cows** are there at the Country Park?

b How many **sheep** are there?

c Sally thought that there were **100** animals at the farm. Explain why Sally was **wrong**.

d Trevor said that there were **at least 110** animals on the farm. Was Trevor correct? Explain your answer.

e **16** horses are brought to the Country Park. Draw what you would add to this pictogram.

4. *You may need tracing paper or a mirror for this question.*

Melanie designed some badges.
All the designs have at least one line of symmetry.
Make a sketch of each design and draw all the lines of symmetry.

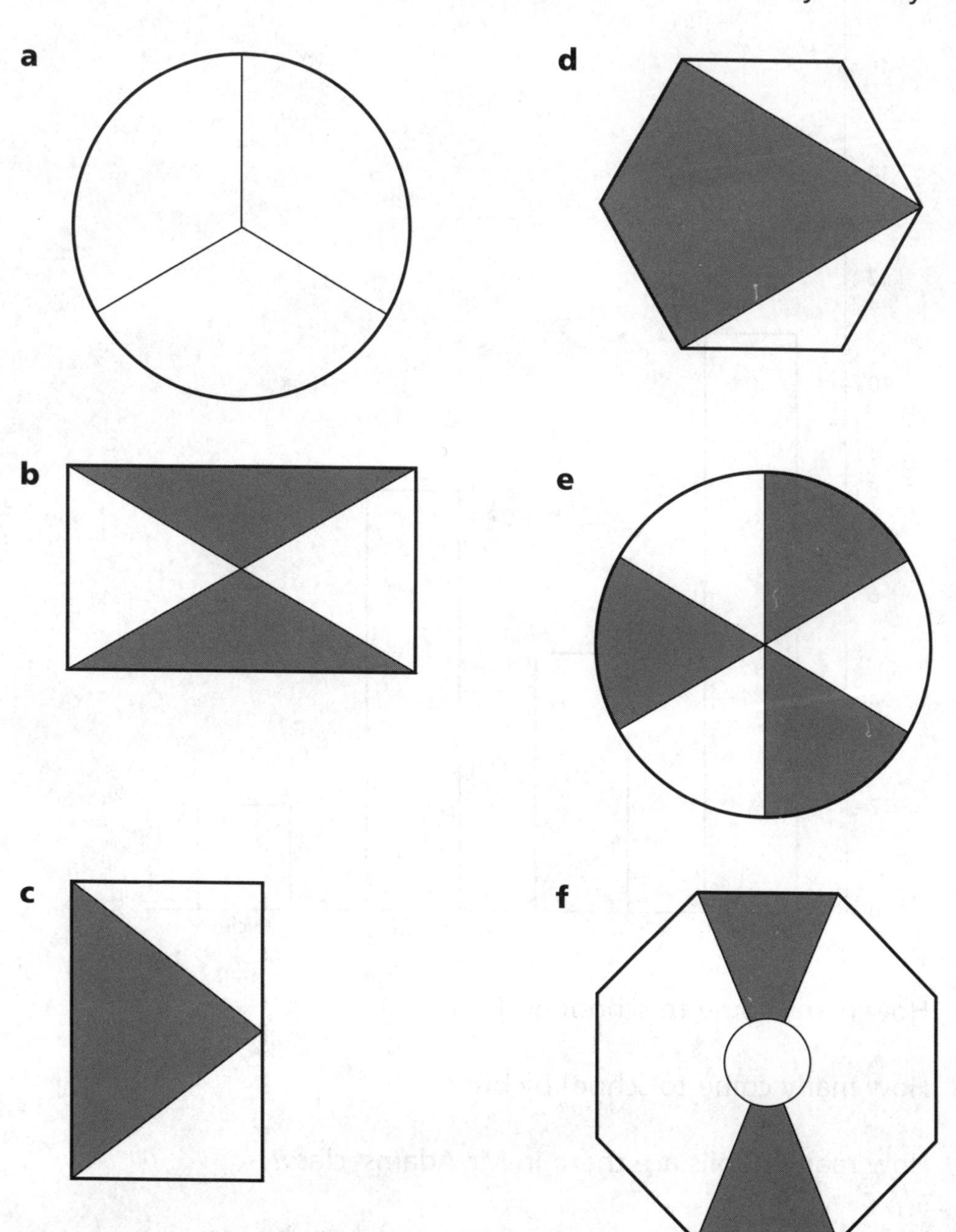

5. Mr Adams asked the students in his class how they came to school. The results are shown on this bar chart.

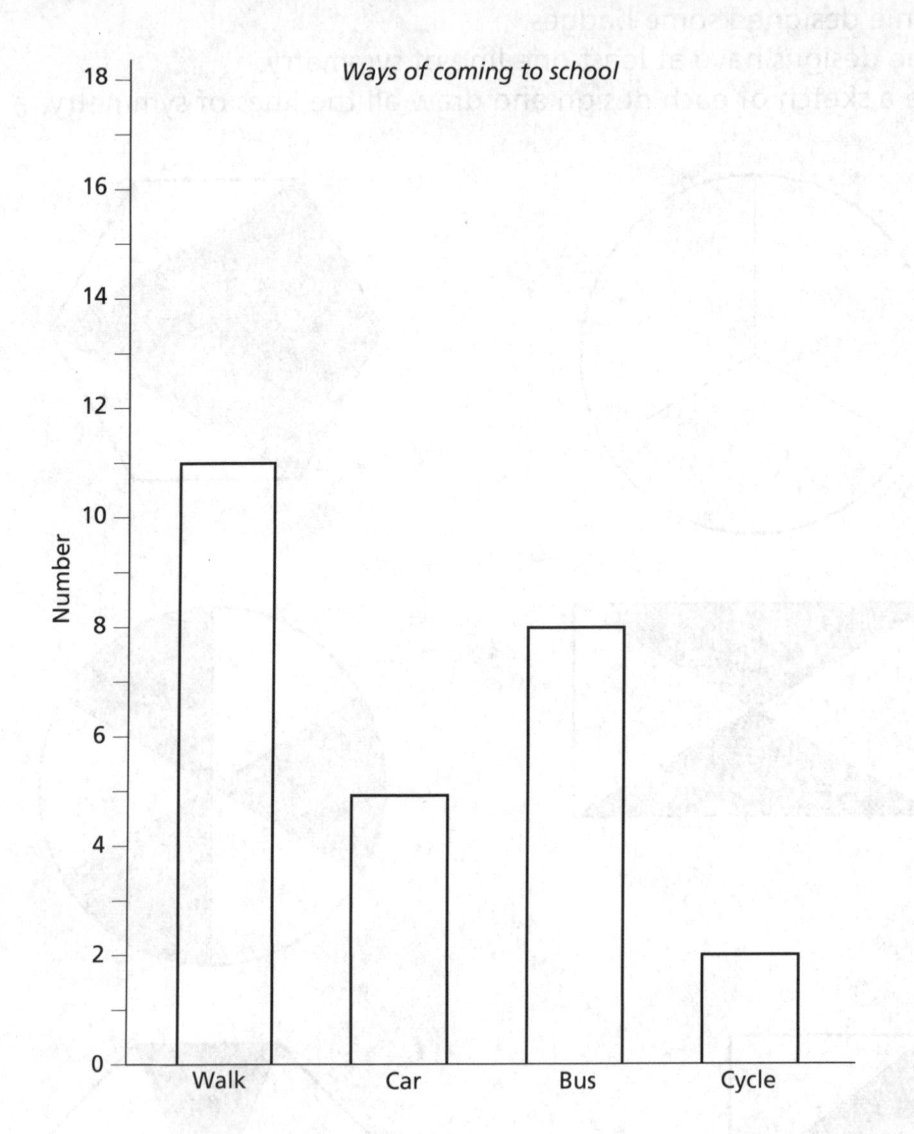

a How many come to school on foot?

b How many come to school by bus?

c How many pupils are there in Mr Adams' class?

d Libby said that twice as many came by bus as by car.
Explain why Libby was wrong.

e Write down another fact that this bar chart tells you.

6. Karin sorted some shapes into two groups.

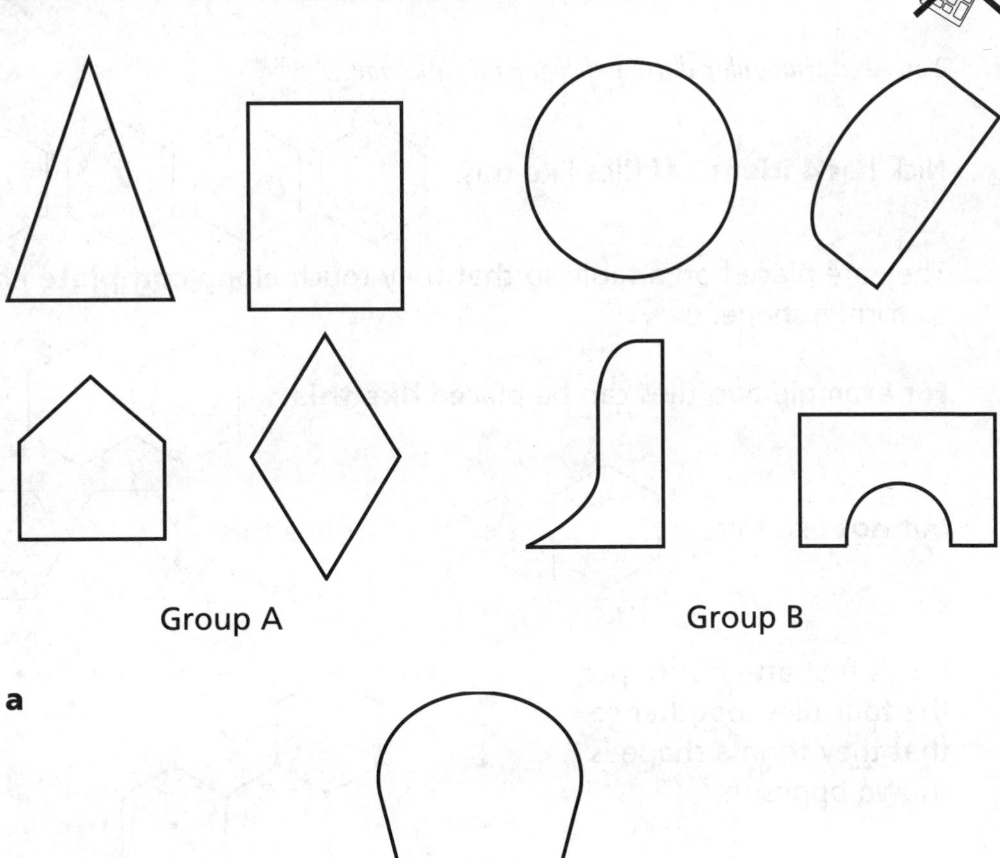

a

Marc said that this shape belonged to Group B.
Explain why Marc was right.

Which group does each of these shapes belong to?

b

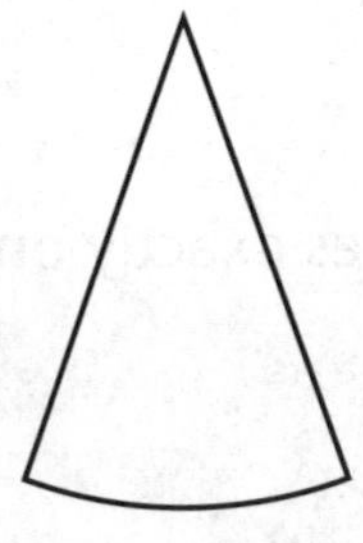

c

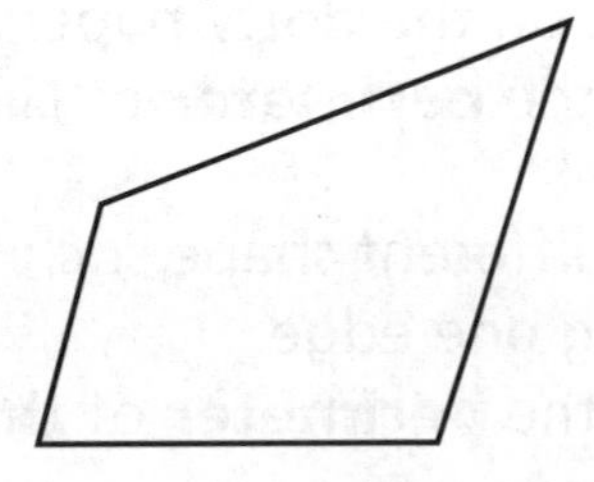

d

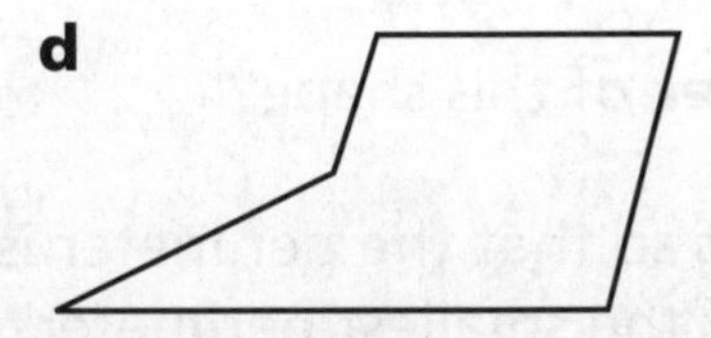

7. *You need triangular dotty paper for this question.*

Nick has **4 identical** tiles like this: 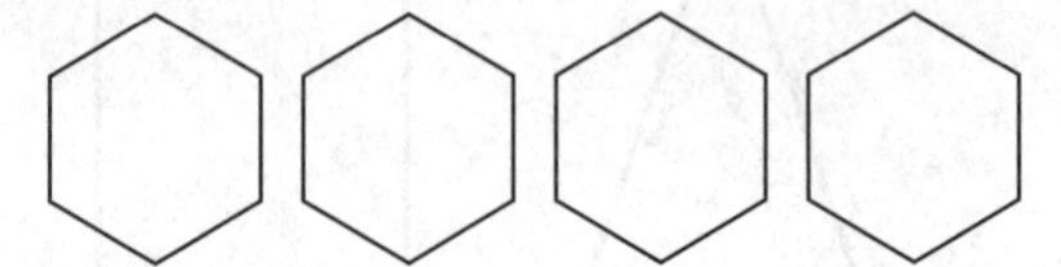

They are placed on a table so that they touch along **complete** edges to form a shape.

For example two tiles can be placed **like this** 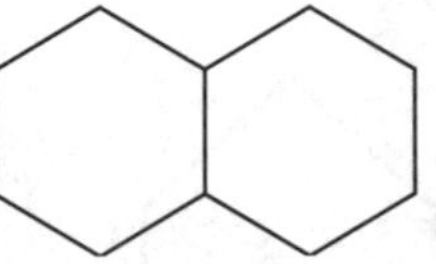

but **not** like this 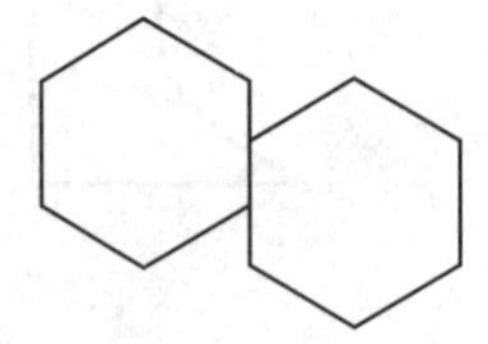 or like this 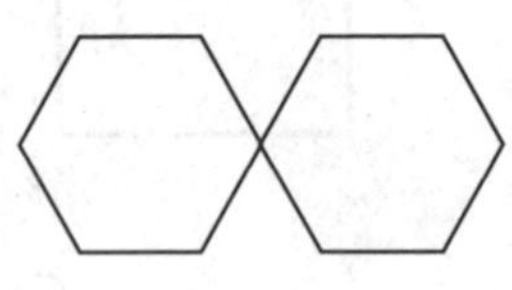

Nick's first attempt to put the four tiles together so that they form a shape is shown opposite.

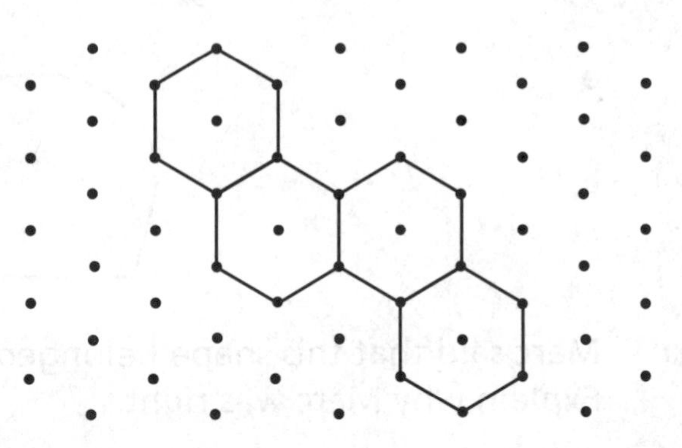

a Draw a shape that is **different** from Nick's first attempt.

b The dots on the dotty paper are **1 cm** apart.
What is the **perimeter** of Nick's first attempt?

c Draw a different shape such that each tile touches exactly one other tile along one edge.
What is the **perimeter** of this shape?

d Draw another shape so that each tile touches exactly one other tile along one edge.
What is the **perimeter** of this shape?

e Arrange the four tiles so that the perimeter is as **small** as possible.
What is the length of the smallest perimeter?

8. The number in any square is the sum of the two numbers in the circles on either side of that square. Copy the diagrams and fill in the missing numbers.

a

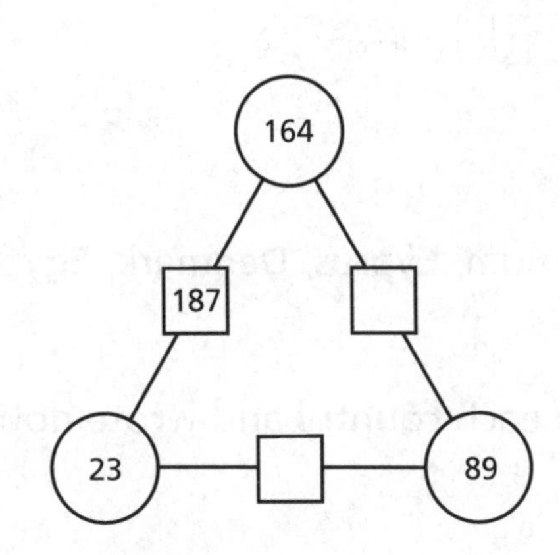

d

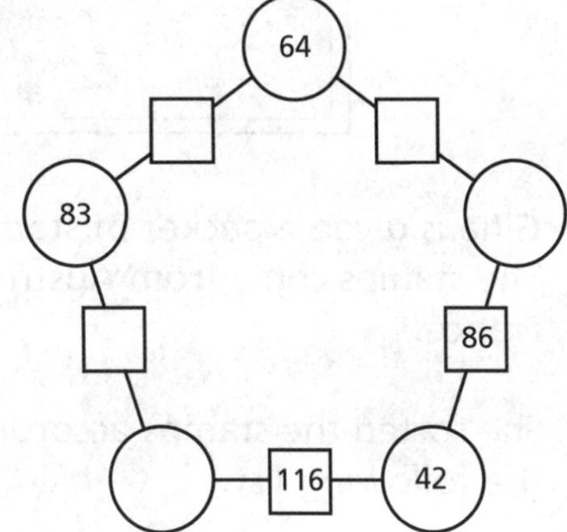

b

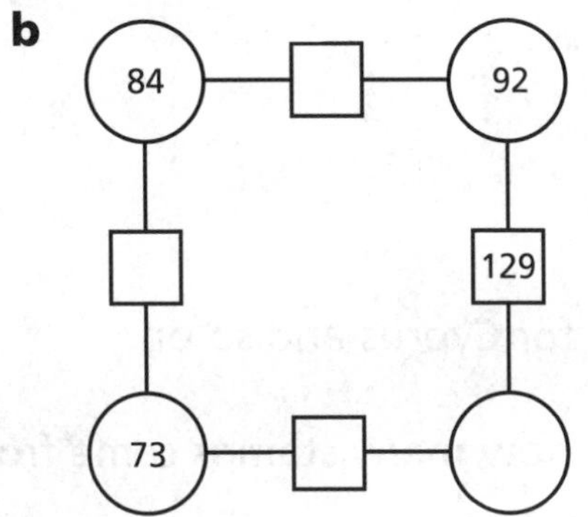

e

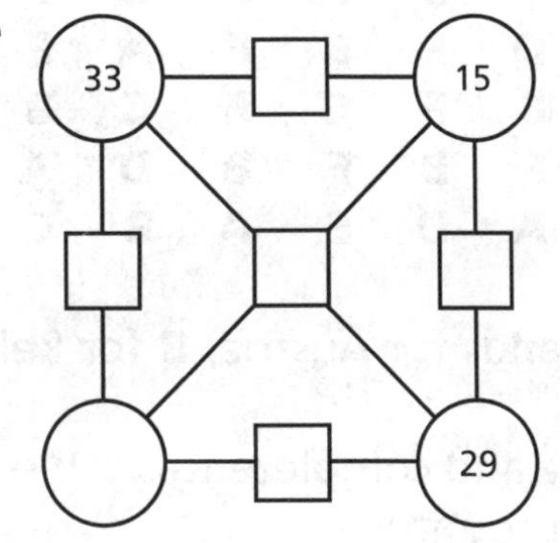

c

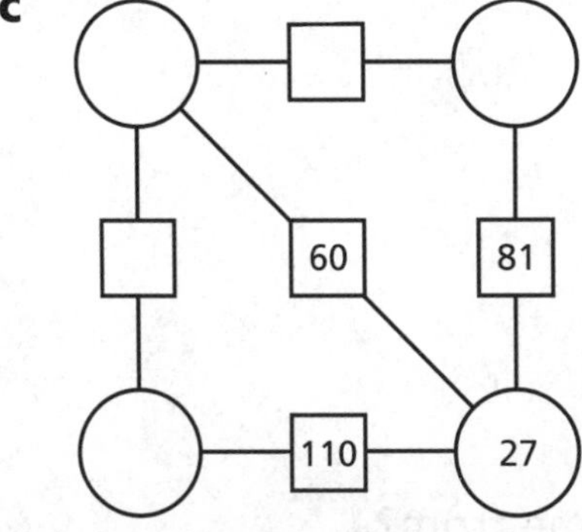

f

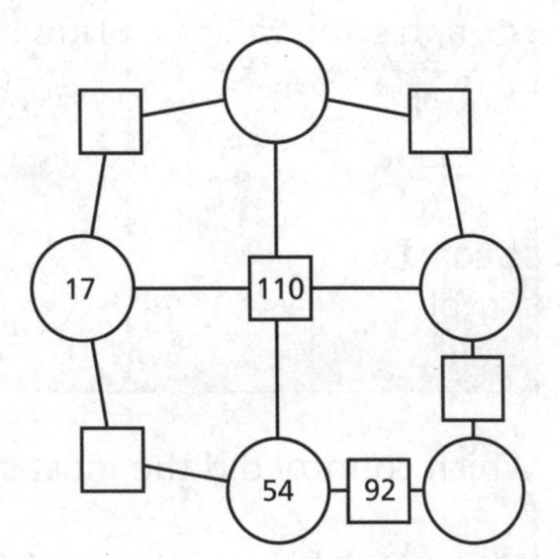

9.

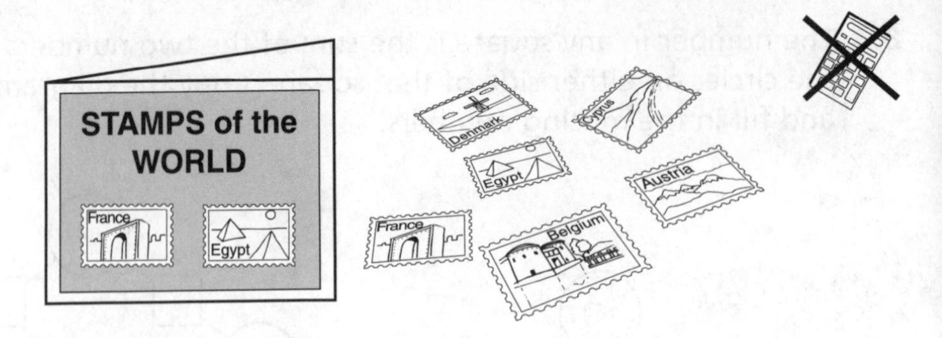

Gina is given a packet of stamps.
The stamps come from Austria, Belgium, Cyprus, Denmark, Egypt and France.

She sorted the stamps according to each country and wrote down the following list.

C B A F D B F
D F B F A F
E F C E C B
F B F B D A
A D E A B C

A stands for Austria, **B** for Belgium, **C** for Cyprus and so on.

a Copy and complete this table to show how many stamps came from each country.

Country	Tally	Number
Austria		
Belgium		
Cyprus		
Denmark		
Egypt		
France		

b Which country did the most stamps come from?

c When Wendy looked at Gina's stamps she thought that the lowest number of stamps came from Cyprus.
How can Gina tell from the table that Wendy was wrong?

10. A greengrocer has three tables for displaying fruit.

a About 25% of this table is used for bananas.

bananas | apples
oranges

About what **percentage** of this table is for **(i)** oranges **(ii)** apples?

b About $\frac{1}{4}$ of this table is for melons.

kiwi fruit | melons | grapefruit
peaches | pineapples

About what **fraction** is for **(i)** grapefruit **(ii)** peaches?

c About $\frac{3}{5}$ of the third table is for pears.

Copy this shape and shade it to show the area for pears.
The rest of the table is for cherries.
Don Said that the area for cherries is about 40%.
Explain why Don is correct.

Level 5 • Questions 11 to 15

11.

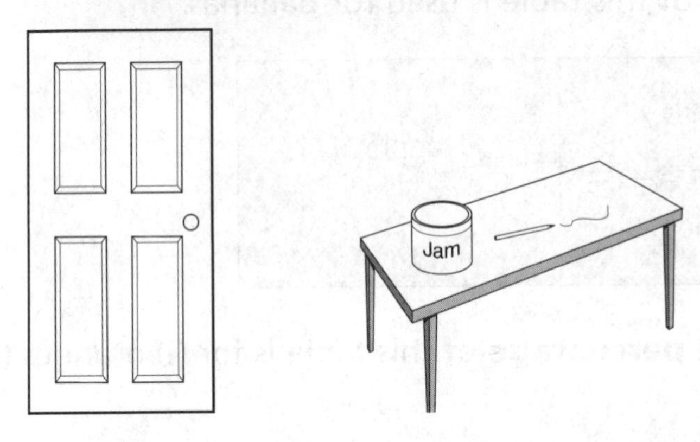

a A door is 196 cm high. How many metres is this?

b The amount of sugar in a tin of jam is 650 g. How many kilograms is this?

c The length of a pencil is 18 cm. How many millimetres is this?

d Sara's best recorded high jump is 1782 mm. How many metres is this?

e Mrs Joyce needs 14 pints of milk for a coffee evening. **About** how many litres is this?

12.

Near the end of a game of *Scrabble* there are six letters still in the bag.

They are 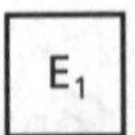

A_1 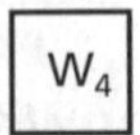

U_1 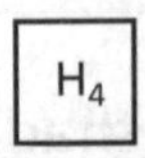

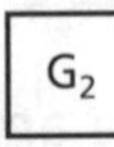

Find the probability that the next letter drawn

a is the letter U

b is a vowel

c is worth 1 point

d is worth more than 1 point.

26 Malcolm has made a design for the centre of a flower garden. It involves laying a square of slabs and adding one slab on each side. The extra slabs will lead to four paths in the garden.

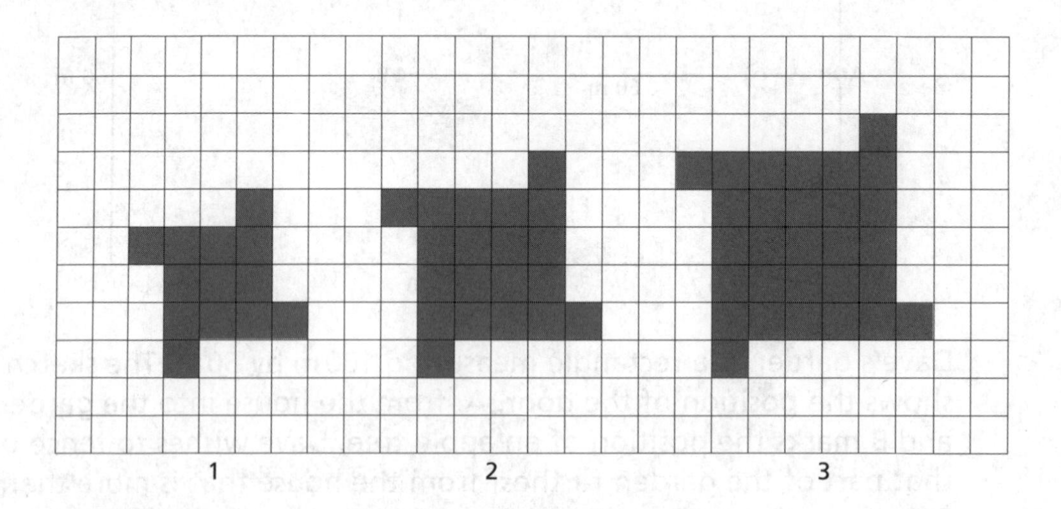

a How many slabs are needed for the 4th design in the pattern?

b How many slabs are needed for the 7th design in the pattern?

c How many slabs are needed for the nth design in the pattern?

d One design uses 148 slabs. What design number is this in the pattern? How many slabs are there along each side of the central square?

e Is there a design number that uses (**i**) 120 slabs (**ii**) 104 slabs? Explain your answer.

f What is the size of the largest central square possible if 140 slabs are available (but not necessarily all used) to lay a design using this pattern?

13.

At *The Orient* take-away **one** piece of cooked chicken breast costs £1.95 and **one** portion of chips costs 85 p.

a Copy and complete this price list.

Chicken	Chips	Price
1	1	£2.75
2	1	£4.70
2	2	
3	2	
3	3	
4	3	
4	4	
5	4	

b The cost, in pounds, of each order is given by the formula

$$\text{cost} = 1.95n + 0.8m$$

where n is the number of pieces of chicken breast
and m is the number of portions of chips.

Use this formula to find the cost of

(i) 6 pieces of chicken **and** 4 portions of chips
(ii) 10 pieces of chicken **and** 6 portions of chips.

14a A school canteen offers five main courses. The table shows the percentage of students who chose *Fish and Chips*, *Cold Meat* and *Cottage Pie* last Wednesday.

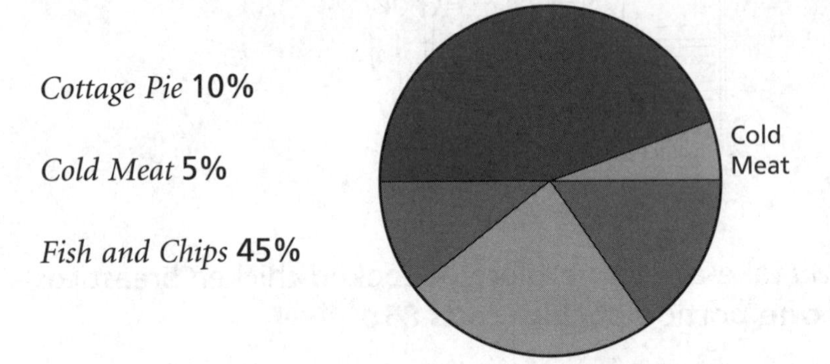

Copy the diagram and label the two sections of the pie chart that represent *Fish and Chips* and *Cottage Pie*.
Cold Meat has already been labelled for you.

b The other two choices were *Sausages* and *Hotpot*.
More students chose *Sausages* than *Hotpot*.
Use the chart to estimate the percentage of students who chose *Sausages*.

c About what percentage of the students chose *Hotpot*?

d Altogether 540 main courses were served on Wednesday.
Copy and complete this table.

Main course		Number of students served
Cottage Pie	10%	
Cold Meat	5%	
Fish and Chips	45%	

e On Wednesday 540 students bought a main course and on Thursday 220 students bought a main course.

On Wednesday 45% of the students chose *Fish and Chips* and on Thursday 60% of the students chose *Fish and Chips*.

Andy argued that since 60% is more than 40%, more students chose *Fish and Chips* on Thursday than on Wednesday.
Explain why Andy is wrong.

15 Several shapes are drawn below on a 1 cm grid.
Find, by counting squares, the area of each shape.

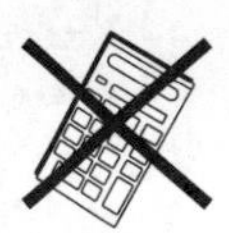

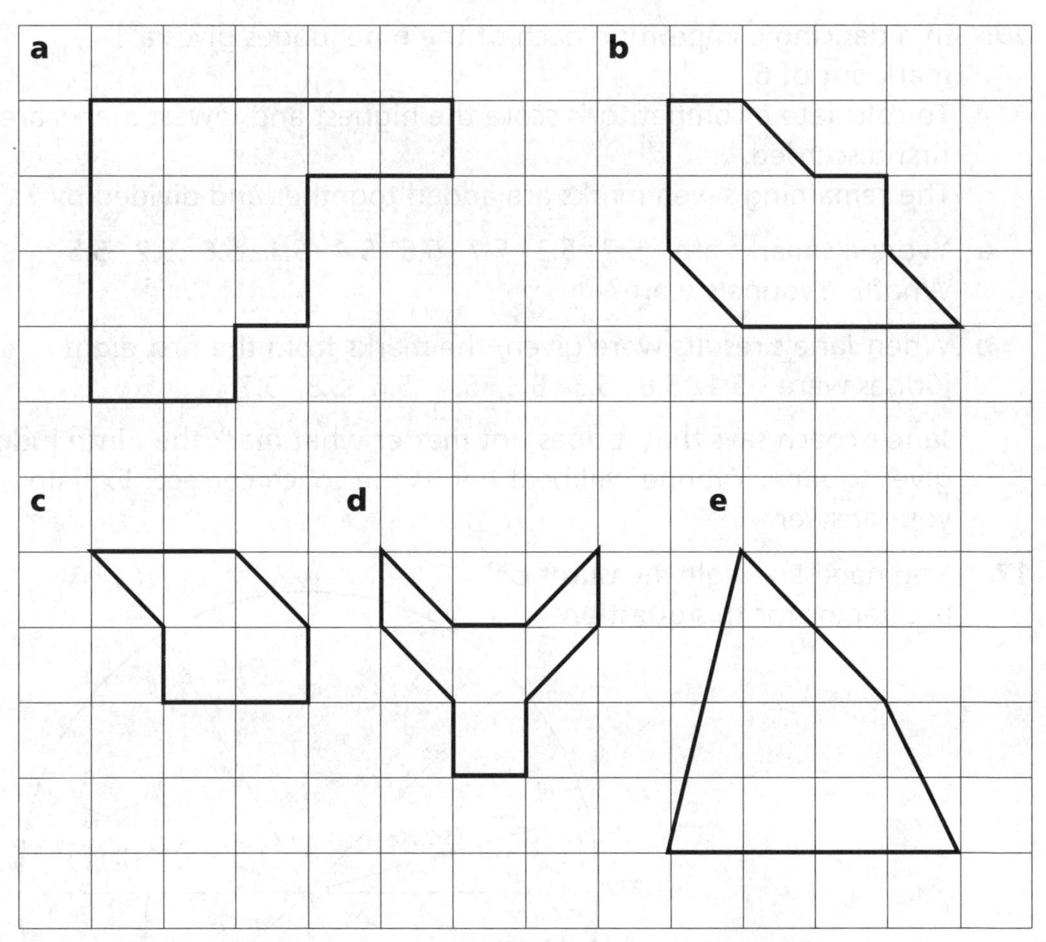

f By counting squares, find the area of this oak leaf, which is drawn on a 1 cm grid. Count a square if more than half of it is within the shape, otherwise do not.

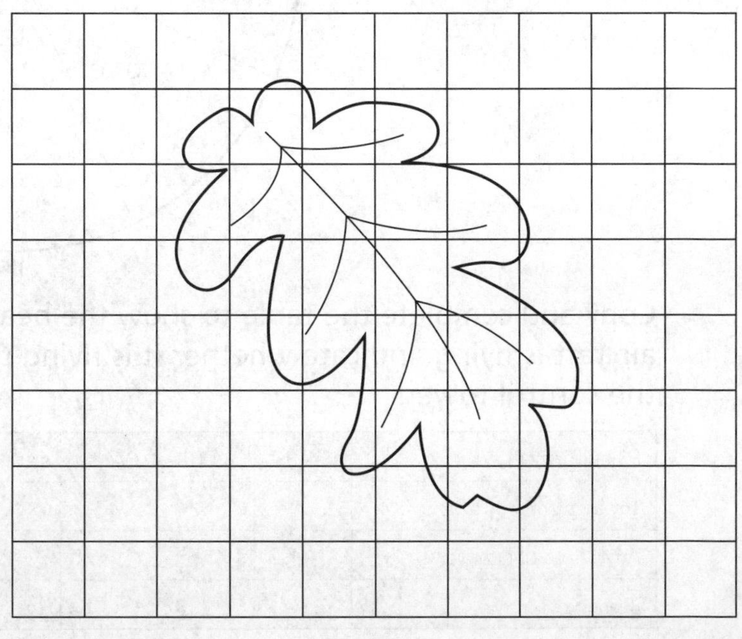

16. In a dancing competition each of the nine judges gives a mark out of 6.
To calculate a competitor's score the highest and lowest marks are first discarded.
The remaining seven marks are added together and divided by 7.

a Yvonne's marks are 5.2 5.3 5.7 5.6 5.4 5.1 5.6 5.2 5.5
What is Yvonne's score?

b When Jane's results were given, the marks from the first eight judges were 5.1 5.6 5.3 5.3 5.4 5.6 5.3 5.7

Jane's coach says that it does not matter what mark the ninth judge gives to Jane, Yvonne will beat her. Is the coach correct? Explain your answer.

17. You need an angle measurer or protractor for this question.

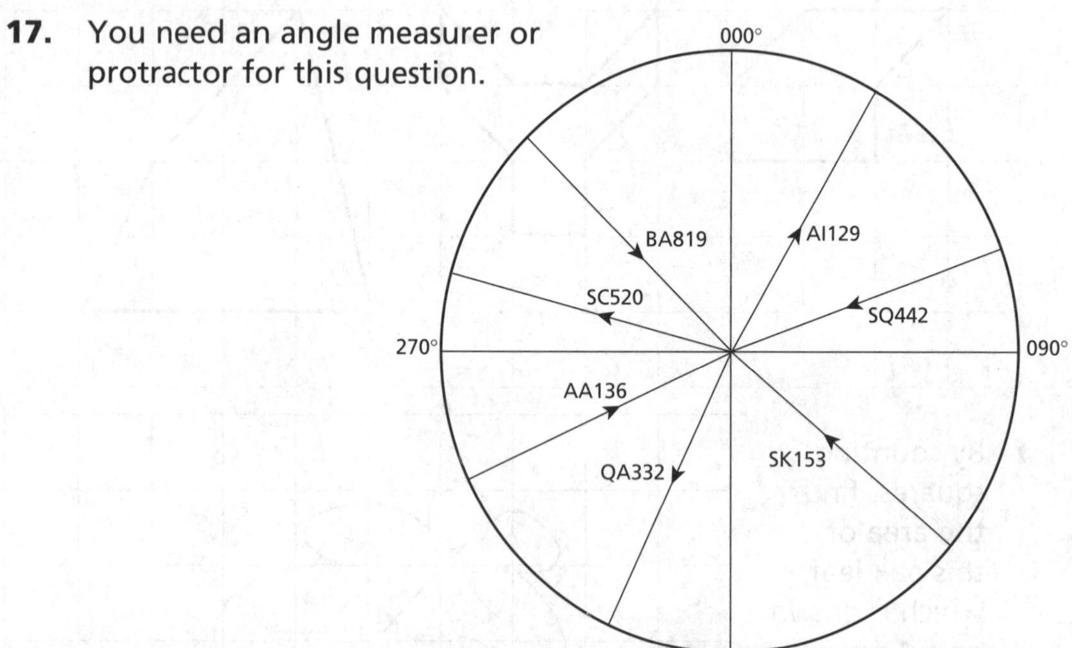

Copy and complete the table to show the bearing on which each aircraft is flying. Indicate whether it is flying towards or away from the control tower.

Flight Number	SK153	BA819	QA332	AI129	AA136	SC520	SQ442
Towards Control Tower	✓						
Away from Control Tower							
Bearing	315°						

18. Griff has a supply of white plastic cubes, each with an edge of 1 cm.
He uses some of them to build this stack of loose cubes.

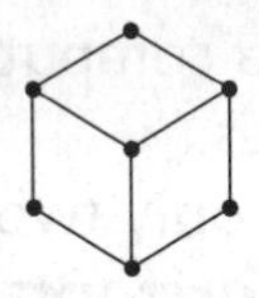

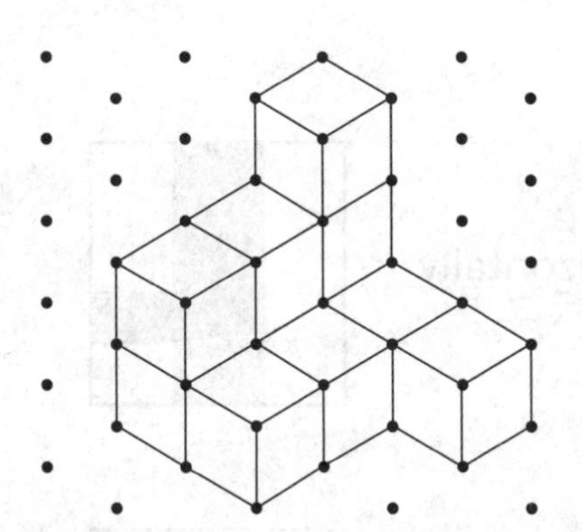

a How many cubes are used to build this stack?

b Find the volume of the stack.

c Find the area of the base of the stack.

d Find the total surface area of the stack including the base.

e How many more cubes are needed to assemble a large solid cube that has an edge of 3 cm?

19. A rectangular piece of card measuring 12 cm by 9 cm is to be used to make a small open rectangular box by cutting out squares from the corners and folding up the sides.

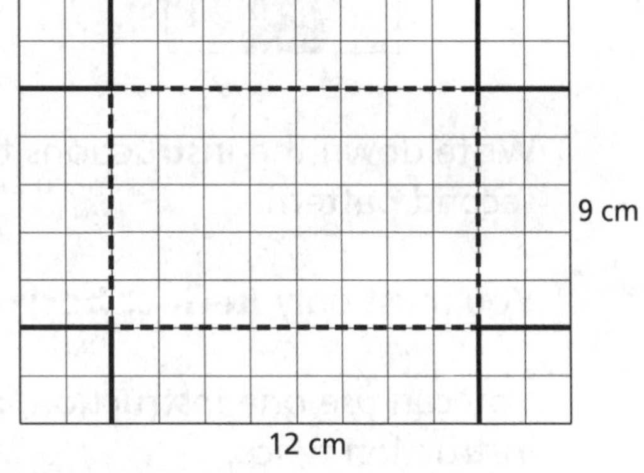

a How many different boxes can be made from this piece of card if the length and breadth of the base is to be a whole number of centimetres?

b For each different box find
(i) its dimensions **(ii)** its total external surface area **(iii)** its capacity.

c Use the information you have found in **b** to state whether each of these statements is true (T) or false (F).

A The box with the largest base has the greatest capacity.
B The box with the smallest total external surface area has the smallest capacity.
C The box with the greatest capacity is as deep as it is wide.

d Find the dimensions of the largest **cubical** open box that can be made from a rectangular card measuring 12 cm by 9 cm if the length of each edge is a whole number of centimetres. How much card is wasted?

20. Ron uses a computer programme to transform shapes on square tiles.
There are only two instructions in the program:
Reflect horizontally or **Rotate 90° clockwise**

For example

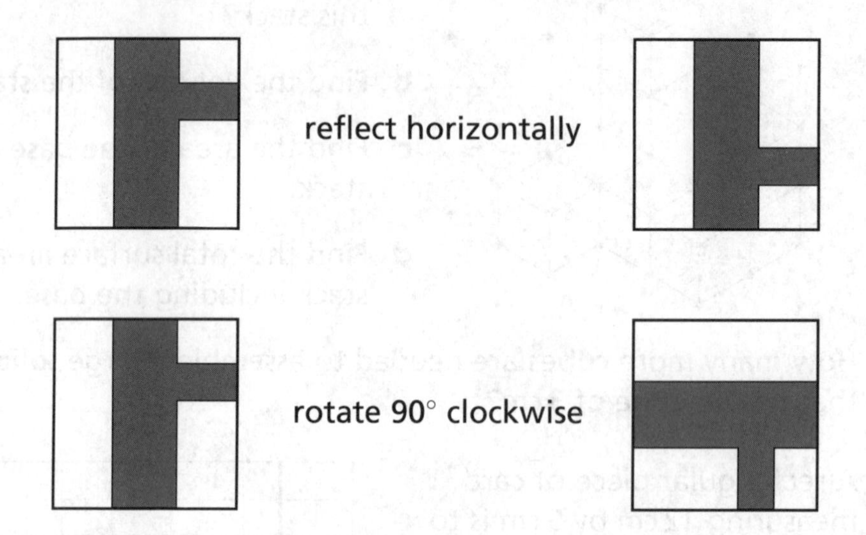

Write down the instructions to transform the first pattern into the second pattern.

You must only **Reflect horizontally** or **Rotate 90° clockwise.**

You can use one instruction, both instructions, or the same instruction twice.

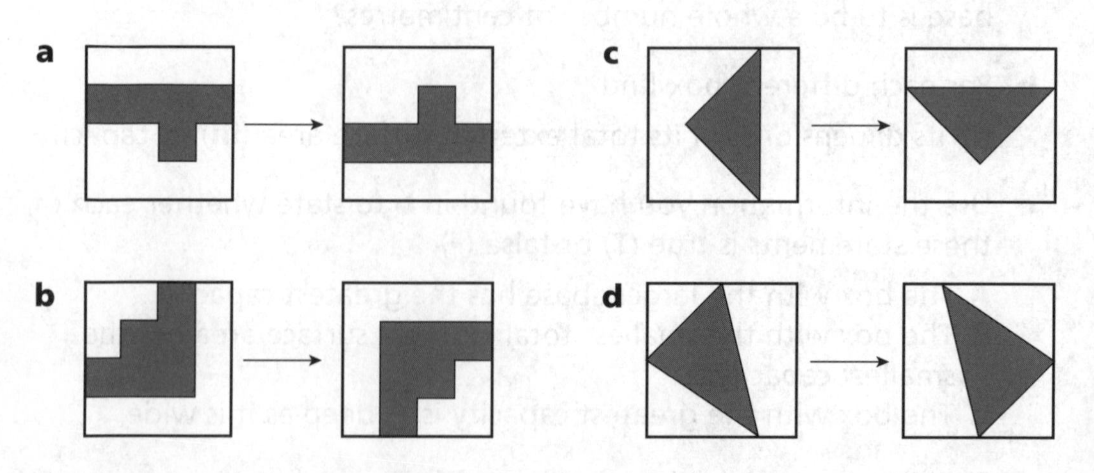

21 A motor company tested 10 cars of the same model which had been manufactured at yearly intervals over a 10-year period.

The first test recorded the number of miles per gallon (m.p.g.) for each car when driven at a steady 40 m.p.h.

The results for this test are given in *Graph A*.

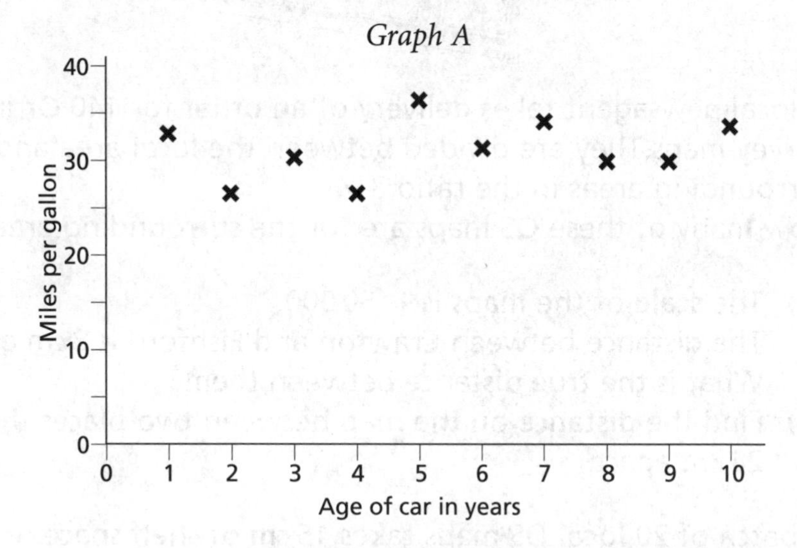

The second test took the same 10 cars and found the miles per gallon when the cars were driven at steady, but different, speeds.

The results are given in *Graph B*.

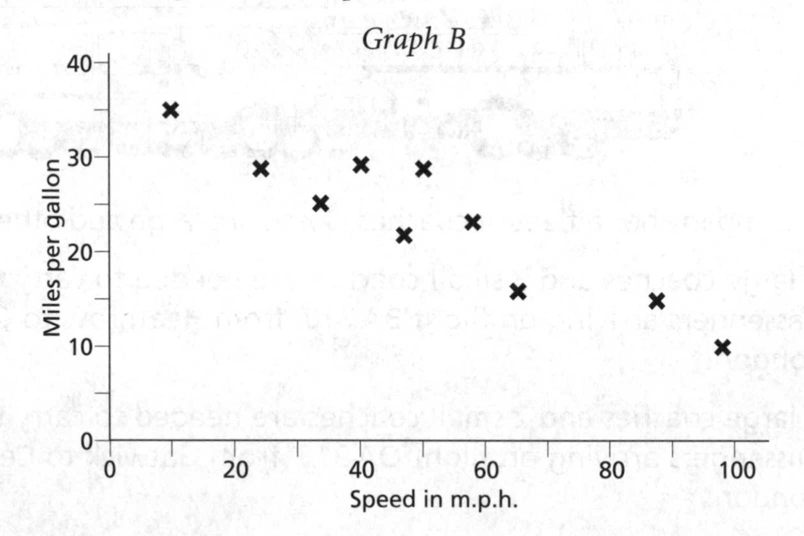

a What does *Graph A* show about the relationship between miles per gallon and the age of the car?

b What does *Graph B* show about the relationship between miles per gallon and the steady speed at which a car is driven?

Level 7 • Questions 22 to 26

22.

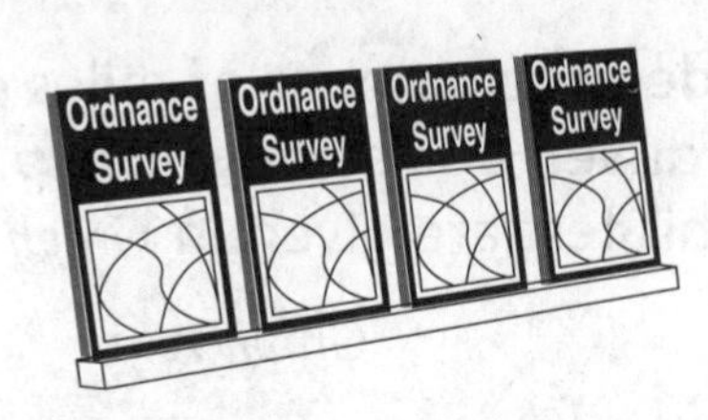

a A local newsagent takes delivery of an order for 140 Ordnance Survey maps.They are divided between the local area and the surrounding areas in the ratio 3 : 4.
How many of these OS maps are for the surrounding areas?

b **(i)** The scale of the maps is 1 : 50 000.
The distance between Crawton and Fishford is 8 cm on the map.
What is the true distance between them?

(ii) Find the distance on the map between two places that are 24 km apart.

c A batch of 20 local OS maps takes 15 cm of shelf space.
What length of shelf space is needed for 34 similar OS maps?

23

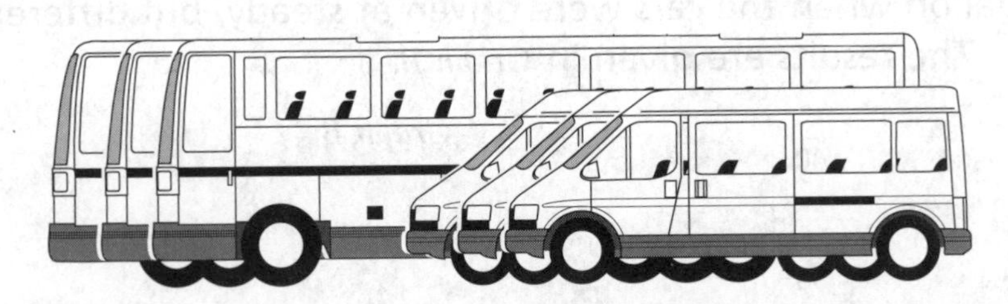

A company has a fleet of coaches. Some are large and others are small.

5 large coaches and 3 small coaches are needed to carry the 307 passengers arriving on flight BA 710, from Heathrow to Central London.

7 large coaches and 2 small coaches are needed to carry the 377 passengers arriving on flight QA 316 ,from Gatwick to Central London.

a If a large coach will carry x passengers and a small coach will carry y passengers form two equations in x and y.

b Solve these equations to find the number of passengers on a large coach.

24. *You need a pair of compasses for this question.*

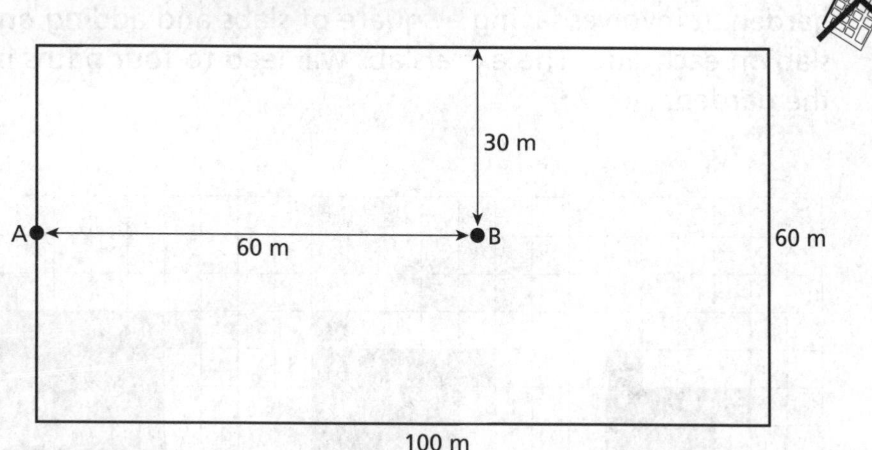

Dave's garden is a rectangle measuring 100 m by 60 m. The sketch shows the position of the door, A, from the house into the garden and B marks the position of an apple tree. Dave wishes to fence off that part of the garden furthest from the house that is more than 50 m from the door and is more than 20 m from the apple tree. Make an accurate drawing of Dave's garden and shade the region that satisfies both conditions.

25. *You need squared paper for this question.*

a Draw x and y axes and scale them from −8 to 8, using 1 cm as 1 unit on both axes.

b Plot the points A(−8, 3), B(0, 7) and C(4, −5).

c Draw the image of △ABC under an enlargement with centre P(−4, −1) and scale factor $\frac{3}{4}$. Label the image A′B′C′.

d Write down the coordinates for A′, B′ and C′.

e What is the relationship between the length of BC, the length of B′C′ and the scale factor?

f How are the directions of BC and B′C′ related?

27.

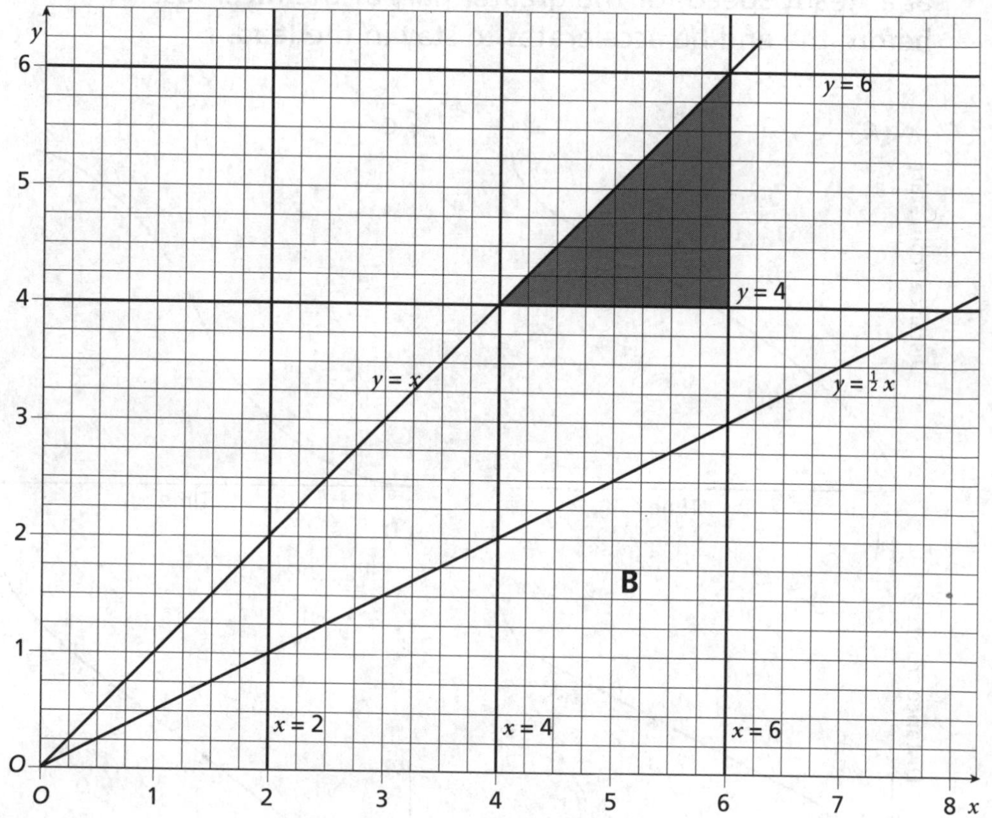

a One region on this diagram can be described by the inequalities

$y \leqslant x$
$y \geqslant \frac{1}{2}x$
$x \geqslant 2$
$x \leqslant 4$

Copy the diagram and put the letter **A** in the region that is described.

b The shaded region can be described using three inequalities. Write down these inequalities.

c Write down as many inequalities as you think are necessary to describe the region marked **B**.

28. Mike is taking part in a cycle race. He begins slowly and accelerates to get into the lead, then settles down to ride at a steady speed for the greater part of the race. Just before the end he accelerates to stay in the lead.

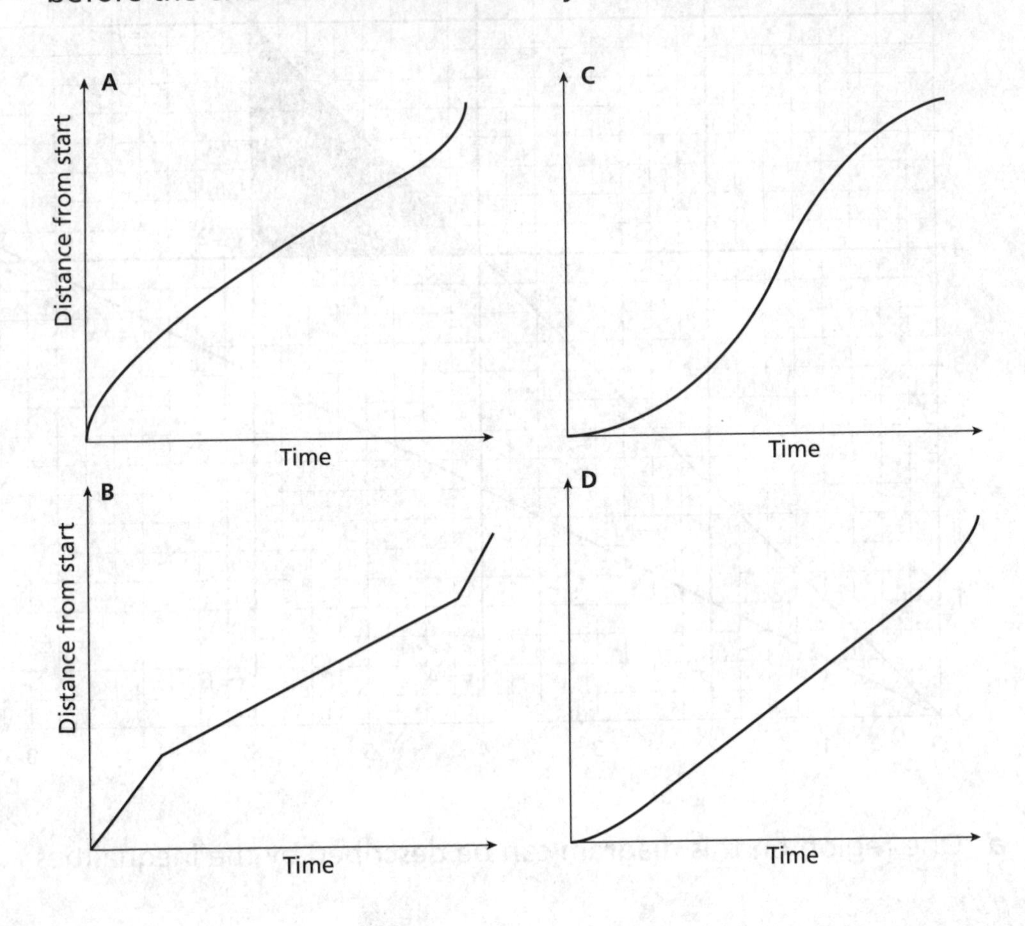

Which of the graphs best represents Mike's ride?

Give a reason why each of the other graphs does not fit the information given.

29. 200 candidates are interviewed for 40 places in a Government Department. Each candidate sits two tests; Test A and Test B.
Test A is marked out of 100 and Test B is marked out of 50.

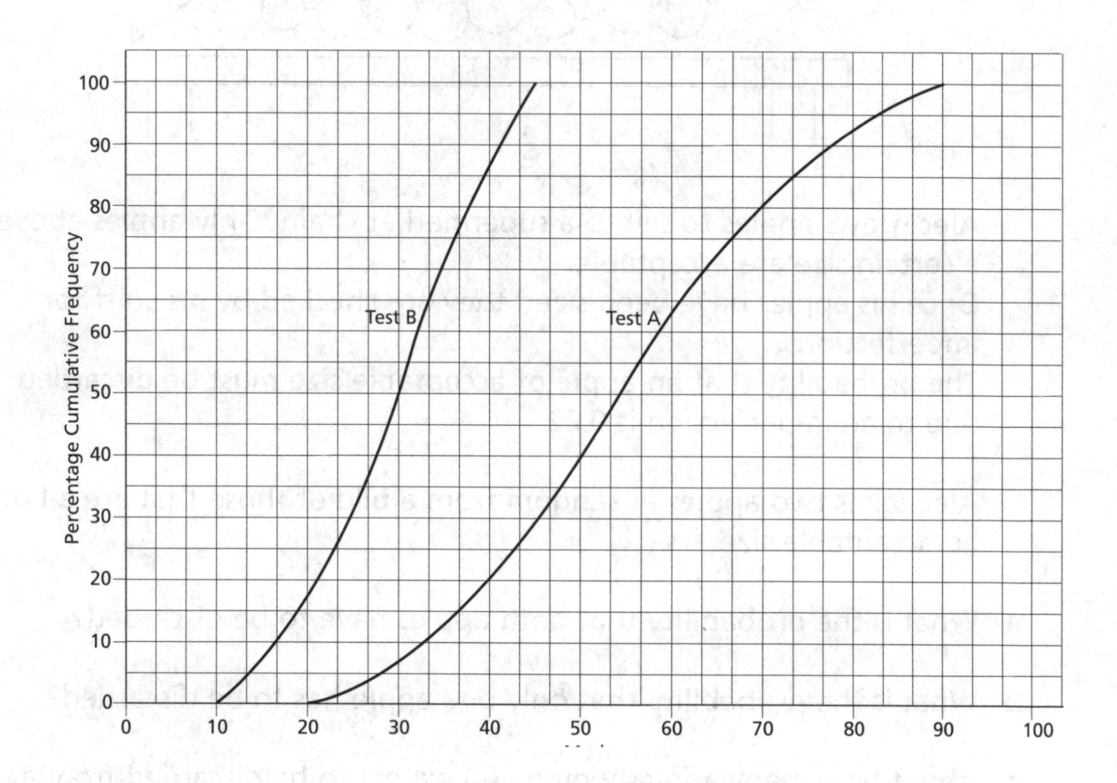

a Use the graph to find the highest mark obtained on **(i)** Test A **(ii)** Test B.

b What is the lowest mark obtained on **(i)** Test A **(ii)** Test B?

c In Test A Gary came first and Edith scored 70. How many places was Edith behind Gary?

d The top 40 candidates on Test A are offered jobs. What is the mark of the lowest candidate accepted?

e Sally scored 65 on Test A. Is Sally likely to be offered one of the 40 places? Explain your answer.

30.

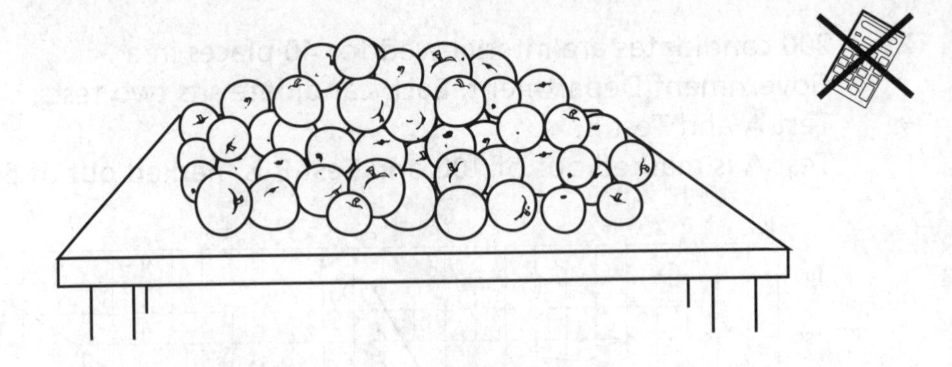

Alec grows apples to sell to a supermarket chain. Only apples above a certain size are acceptable.
Once his apples have been sized they are checked by his staff for imperfections.
The probability that an apple of acceptable size must be discarded due to an imperfection is 0.02.

Alec takes two apples at random from a pile of those that are all of an acceptable size.

a What is the probability that both apples have to be discarded?

b What is the probability that only one apple has to be discarded?

c About how many apples would you expect to be discarded from a pile of 1500?

TEST 1 Paper 2

Calculators may be used for this test.

Level 3 • Questions 1 to 6

1a Reg writes a cheque for **ninety-three pounds thirty-seven pence** to pay his electricity bill.
What figures should he write in the box?

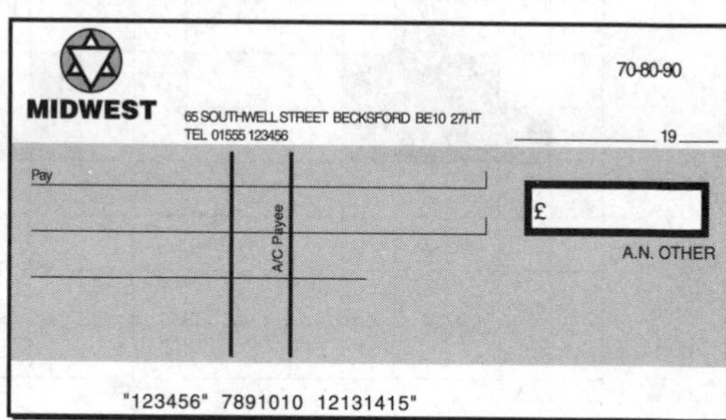

b To pay for a pressure cooker John writes **87.05** in the box after the £ sign. Write this amount in words.

2.

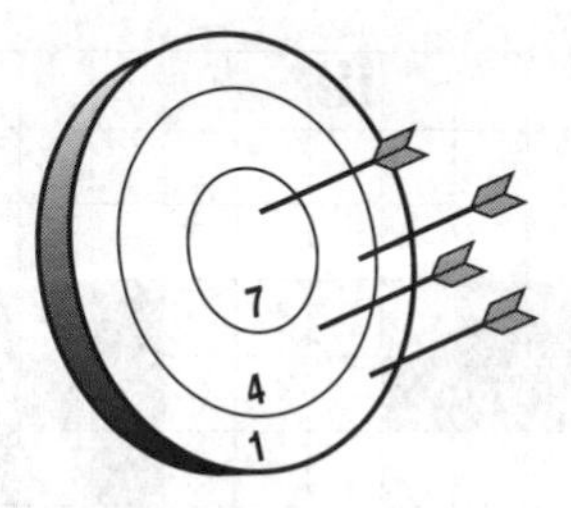

Nia's turn

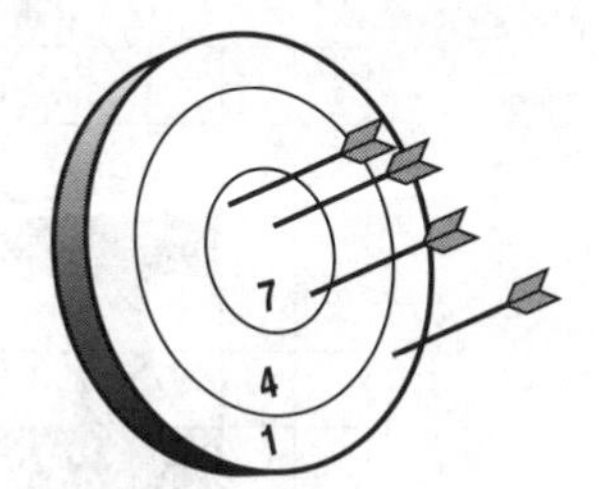

Malcolm's turn

Nia and Malcolm are firing arrows at a target.

a How many points did Nia score?

b How many points did Malcolm score?

c Who had the **higher** score, and by how much?

d Sam scored 19 points with four arrows.
How many of Sam's arrows scored **(i)** 7 points **(ii)** 4 points **(iii)** 1 point?

e What is the **highest** score Wendy can get with four arrows?

f Zena scores 7 points with four arrows. Every arrow scores at least 1 point. Show how Zena's score can total 7.

3.

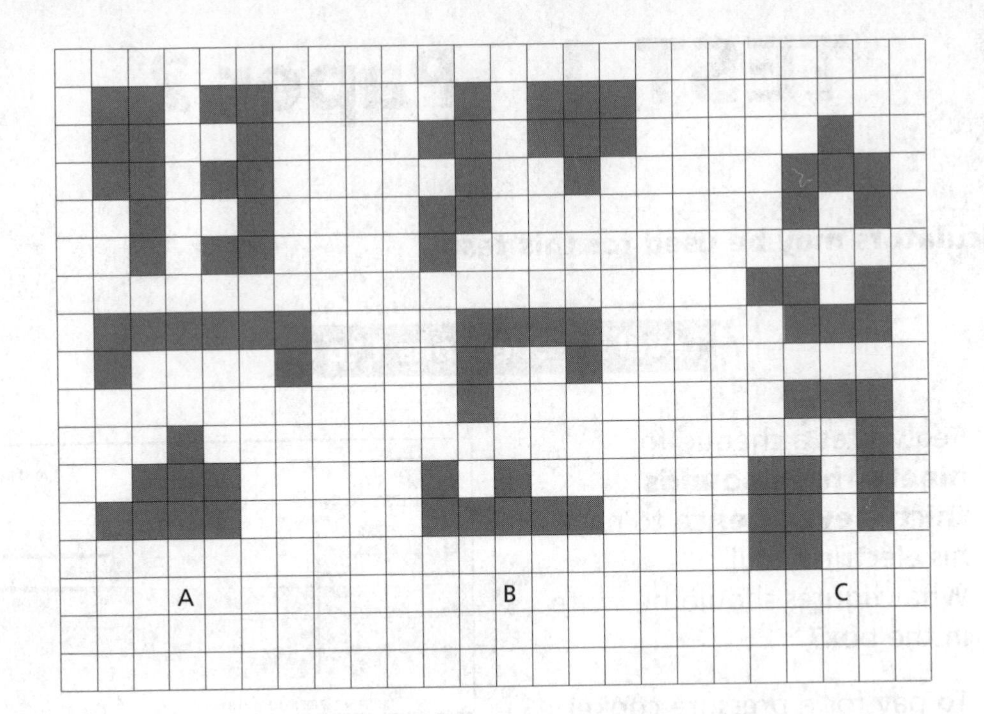

a Which of the sets A, B or C does each of the following shapes belong to?

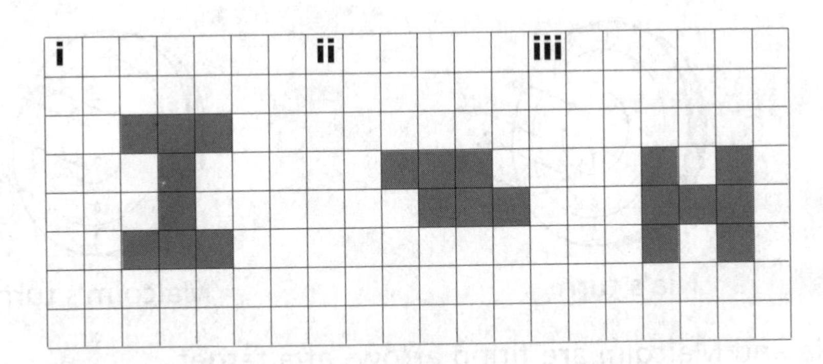

b

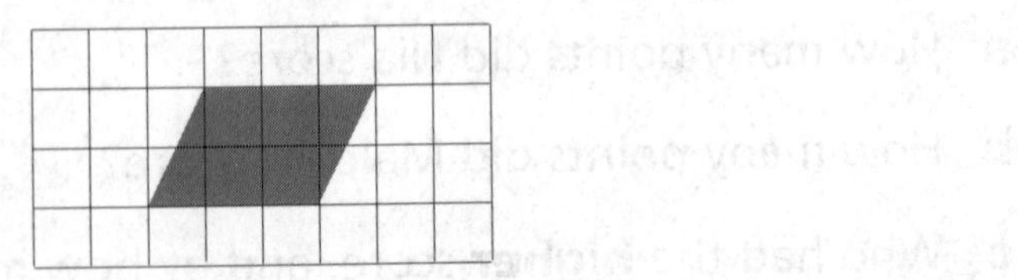

Stan says that this shape belongs to Set C.
Glen says that it doesn't belong to any one of the three given sets.
Who is correct?
Give a reason for your answer.

4.

N

First Avenue Second Avenue Third Avenue

13 14 15 16 17 18

7 8 9 10 11 12

1 2 3 4 5 6

Row 1 Row 2 Row 3 Row 4 Row 5 Row 6

Sections of land on a new housing estate are given **plot numbers.**

Plot 7 is on the **left** as you walk north along First Avenue while **plot 10** is on the **right** as you walk north along Second Avenue.

a What is the number of the plot that is

(i) **6th** on the **right** as you walk north along **First** Avenue
(ii) **9th** on the **left** as you walk north along **Second** Avenue?

b Write down the plot numbers of the next **three** plots on the **right** as you walk north along **Third** Avenue.

c In which avenue would you find **plot 64**?
What are the plot numbers on **each side** of plot **64** on the same side of the street?
What is the plot number **facing Plot 64** on the **opposite** side of the street?

d The **last** plot on the left on **First** Avenue is number **67**.
How many plots are there on **this side** of **First** Avenue?

5.

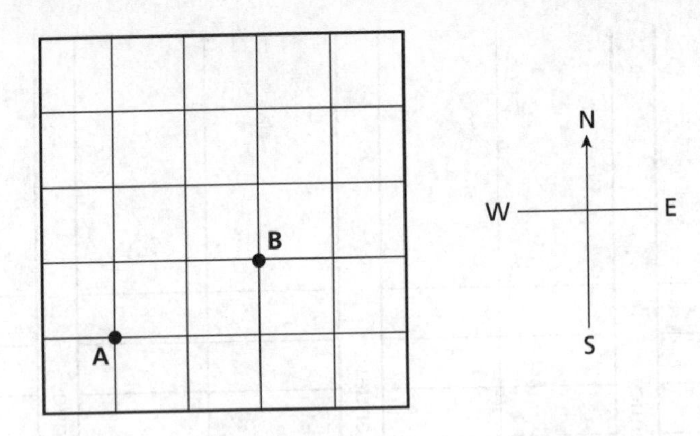

The grid shows part of the road layout in an American city.
A car is at the intersection marked **A**.
Each block of buildings is square and is surrounded by four roads.
One route to go **from A to B** is

2 blocks east followed by **1 block north**.

The distance travelled is described as 3 blocks.

a Give two other routes **from A to B** that travel the same distance.

A taxi wants to travel **from B to A** by a shortest route. At each intersection it must go **south** or **west**.

b How many possible routes are there?

c Describe each route like the route is described in part **a**.

d How many blocks is the length of each shortest route?

e Is it possible to travel from **A to B** by a route that is exactly 4 blocks long? If it is, describe such a route.

6. Paula and Judy compared the times they went to bed last night and the times they got up this morning.
Paula said that she went to bed at 10.30 p.m. and got up at 7.15 a.m.
Judy said she went to bed at 22.20 and got up at 08.10.

a Who went to bed first?

b Convert Judy's times to a.m./p.m. times.

c How long was Paula in bed?

d How long was Judy in bed?

e Who was in bed the longer and by how much?

7. Copy this table and complete it so that the quantities listed in *Box A* are matched with the most appropriate measurement given in *Box B*. One pairing is already done for you.

Box A	1	2	3	4	5	6	7	8	9	10	11	12
Box B	G											

Box A	*Box B*
1 capacity of a teaspoon	A 140 ml
2 weight of a new born baby	B 10 litres
3 height of a street lamp	C 1 cubic metre
4 weight of a lorry	D 1.5 metres
5 height of a dining table	E 50 g
6 diameter of the face of a wristwatch	F 3 m
7 capacity of a teacup	G 5 ml
8 capacity of a bucket	H 10 t
9 capacity of a home freezer	I 75 cm
10 height of the ceiling in a house	J 3 cm
11 length of a dining table	K 3 kg
12 weight of a letter	L 10 m

8. Sean has a pack of cards. He picks the three cards shown and arranges them to give the number 783.

7 8 3

a What is the largest number Sean can make by putting these three cards in a row?
What is the smallest number?

b Lou chooses these six cards from Sean's pack.

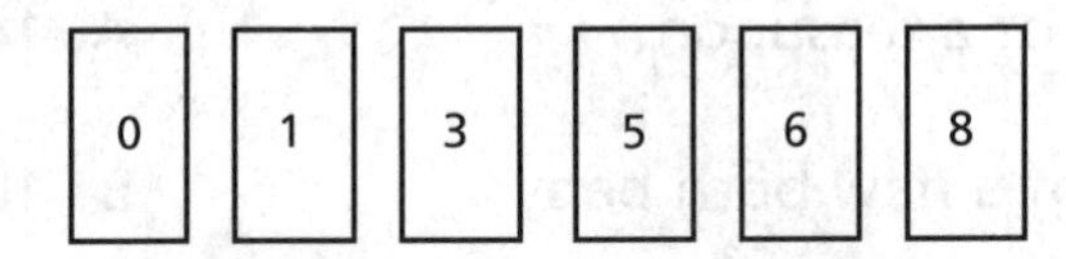

Which cards should he choose to make the largest 3-digit number?
What is that number?
Which other card is needed to make a number that is ten times as large as Lou's 3-digit number?

c Jen has these cards:

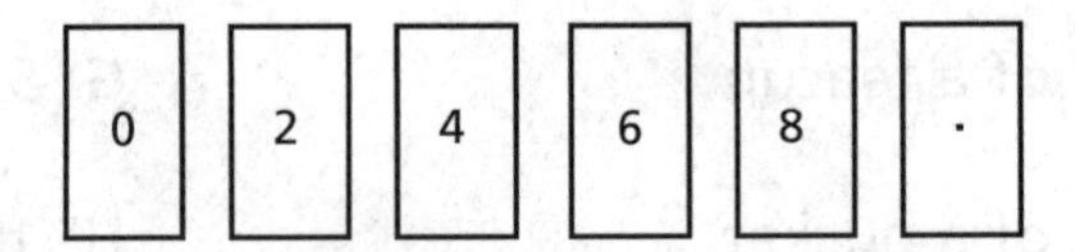

With four cards she made the number 6 4 . 8
Which four cards should Jen use to make a number that is 100 times as large?
What is that number?

d Karen has these cards:

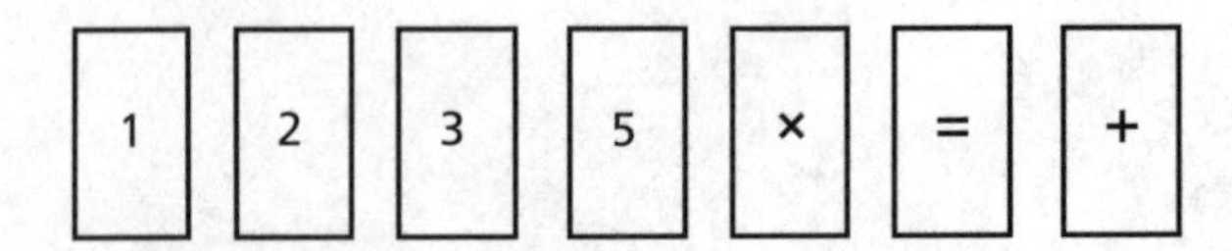

Write down a calculation that uses each card once and only once.

9.

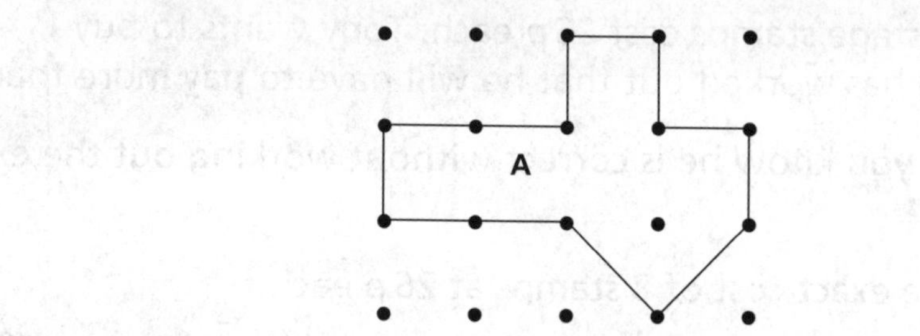

Which of these shapes are congruent with **A**?

10. First class postage stamps cost 26 p each. Tony wants to buy 8 stamps. He has worked out that he will have to pay more than £2.

a Explain how you know he is correct without working out the exact amount.

b Work out the exact cost of 8 stamps at 26 p each.

c Tony was given the 8 stamps in two groups of 4. They were arranged

and

He wondered how many other different ways 4 stamps could be attached to each other.
How many can you find? Draw a sketch of each one.

d Would the answer to **c** be different if he bought the commemorative stamps shown opposite? Explain your answer.

11.

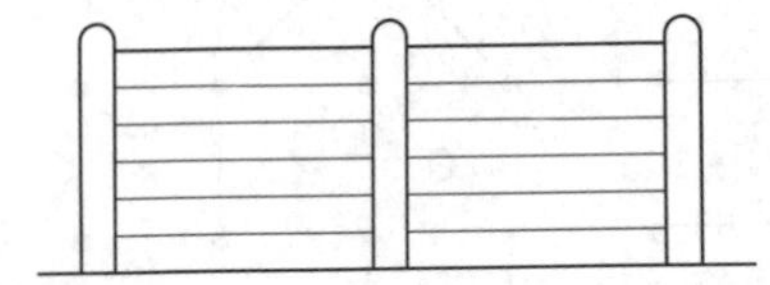

A fence at the side of a motorway is made of concrete posts with horizontal slabs placed between them. 6 slabs are used between any two posts.
If there are 3 posts 12 slabs are needed.

a Copy and complete this table.

Number of posts	Number of slabs
2	6
3	12
4	
5	
6	
8	
10	

b Kevin says that if there are 12 posts there must be 65 slabs. Without working it out explain why Kevin must be wrong.

c Jane says that if there are 36 slabs there must be 7 posts. Explain why Jane is correct.

12. Nick has a collection of school textbooks.
He has n geography books.

a Nick has twice as many history books as geography books.
How many history books does he have?

b Nick has 8 more English books than he has geography books.
How many English books does he have?

c Nick has 2 fewer maths books than he has geography books.
How many maths books does he have?

d How many school textbooks does Nick have altogether for these four subjects? Write your answer as simply as possible.

13.

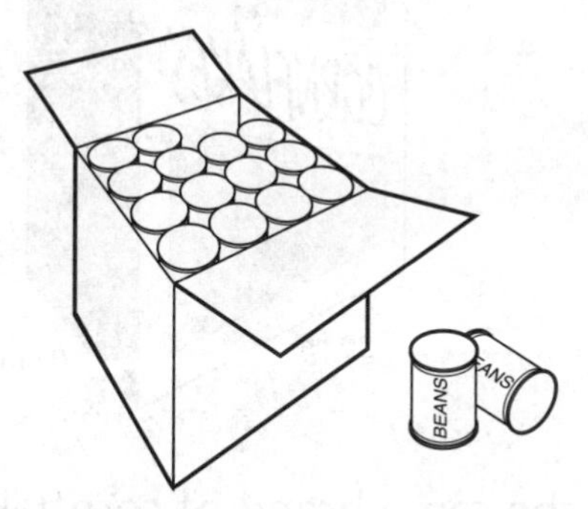

A carton containing 48 tins of beans weighs 21 kg including the packaging. The packaging weighs 840 g.

a How much do the 48 tins of beans weigh altogether?

b How much does 1 tin of beans weigh?

c The greatest load that Brett can carry in his van is 500 kg.
What is the largest number of cartons of beans that he can safely load on to his van?

d The tins are 7.5 cm wide and 10.6 cm high.
How many tins of beans can Jan store side by side in a row on a shelf that is 1.4 m wide?

14a

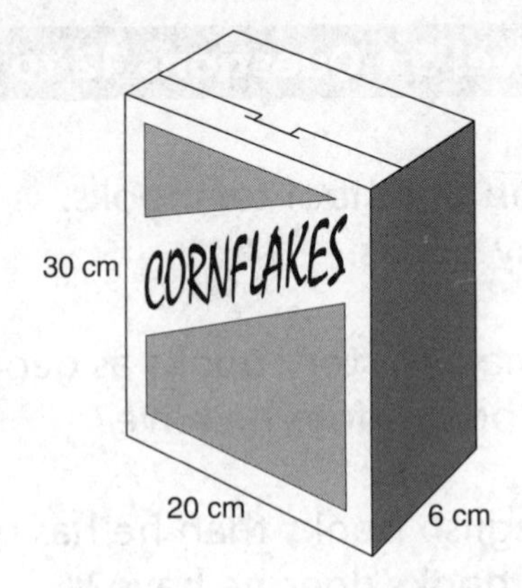

What is the capacity of this standard size box of cornflakes?
Give your answer in cm^3.

b

In a special offer the same brand of cornflakes is sold in a box containing '10% extra'. What is the capacity of this box?

c The standard box holds 500 g.
One normal serving is 25 g.
How many normal servings can be made from

(i) a standard box **(ii)** a 'special offer' box?

15. A family of 10 sit down to Christmas dinner.
In front of every person is a Christmas cracker.
Each cracker contains a paper hat.
Altogether there are two hats of each of the colours red, white, green, blue and yellow.

a Mary likes all the colours except blue.
What is the probability that in her cracker is a hat in a colour that she likes?

b Peg likes all five colours.
What is the probability that she gets a hat in a colour she likes?

c Reg wants a purple hat.
What is the probability that he gets one?

Copy this scale and use it for parts **d** to **g**.

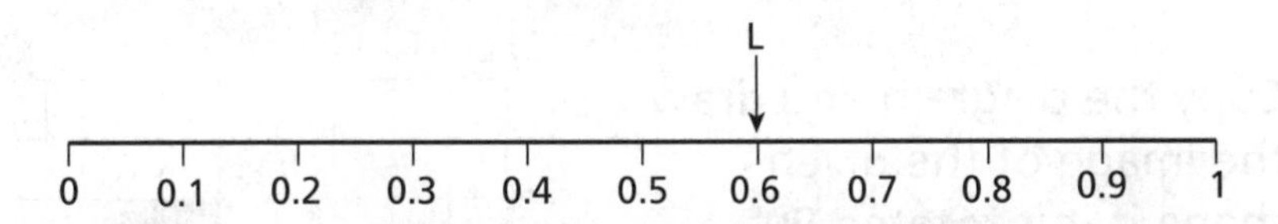

d Mark with an arrow the point on the scale to show the probability that Mary gets a hat of a colour that she likes.
Label it M.

e Draw an arrow to show the probability that Peg gets a hat of the colour she likes.
Label it P.

f Mark with an arrow the point on the scale which shows the probability that Reg gets a hat of a colour that he likes.
Label it R.

g One point on the scale is labelled L.
This shows the probability that Lance gets a hat of a colour that he likes.
Write a sentence that could describe which colours Lance likes.

16. *In this question you can use a mirror or tracing paper if it helps you.*

a Alun has shaded five squares on squared paper.

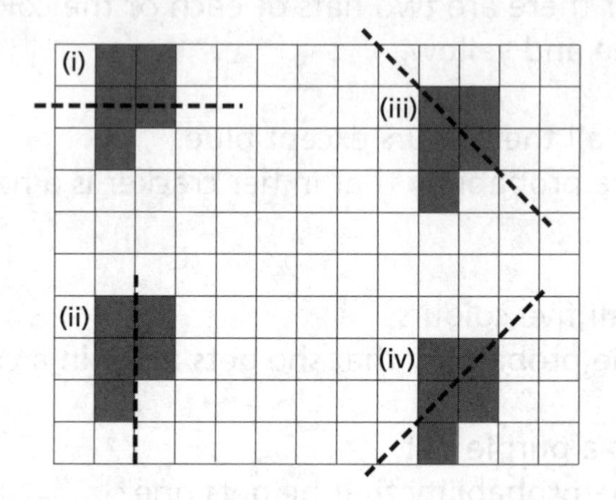

Copy each diagram and shade one more square to make a shape that is symmetrical about the broken line.

b Copy the diagram and draw the image of the given shape if it is rotated 90° clockwise about the point marked **X**.

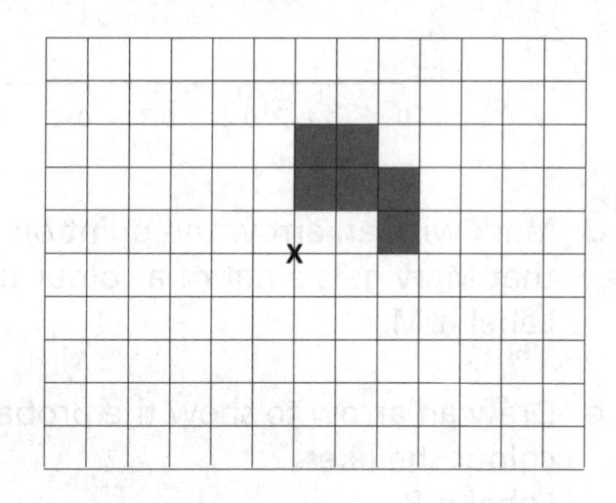

c Copy the diagram and draw the image of the given shape if it is rotated 90° anticlockwise about the point marked **X**.

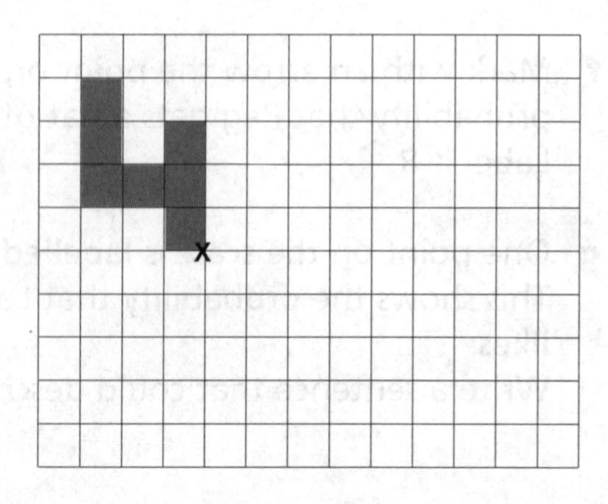

17. The ingredients for 12 scones include

30 g sultanas, 240 g flour, 60 g margarine and 30 g sugar

a Copy and complete the following ratios for the weights of the various quantities.

sultanas : flour : margarine : sugar = 1 :   :   :

b What percentage of the total weight of these ingredients is margarine?

c What fraction of the total weight of these ingredients is flour?

d The ingredients for another recipe, which needs the same amount of sugar included

25% more flour

50% fewer sultanas

and $\frac{2}{3}$ the amount of margarine.

How much of each ingredient is required?

Copy and complete the ratios for the weights of the various ingredients in this recipe.

sultanas : sugar : flour : margarine = 1 :   :   :

18. The instructions to draw this rectangle are

Forward 12 cm
Turn right 90°
Forward 8 cm
Turn right 90°
Forward 12 cm
Turn right 90°
Forward 8 cm

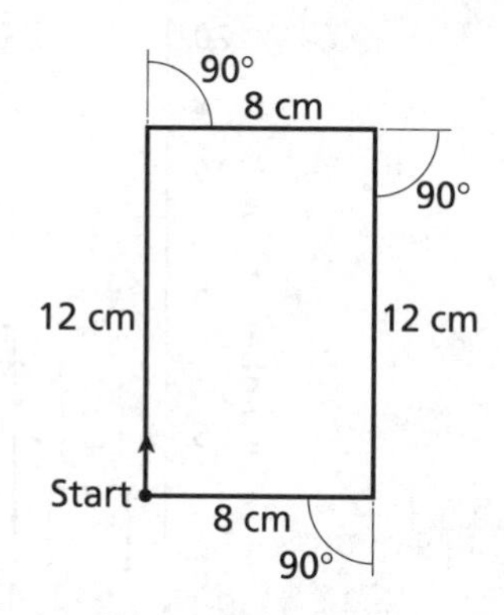

a Write instructions to draw a rectangle whose sides are half the length of the given rectangle.

b Complete the instructions to draw this parallelogram.

Forward 10 cm
Turn left 60°

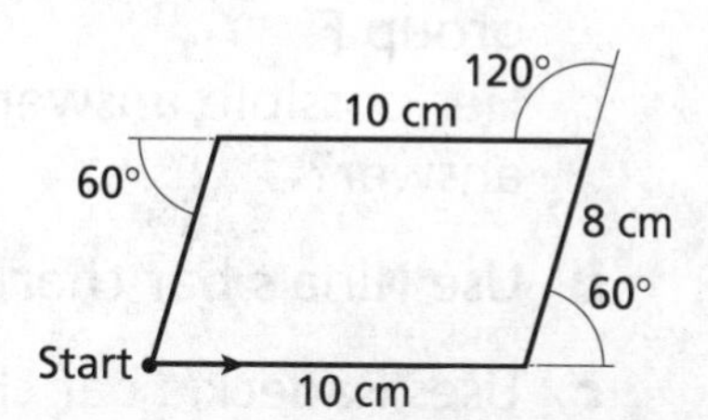

c Give instructions to draw this triangle.

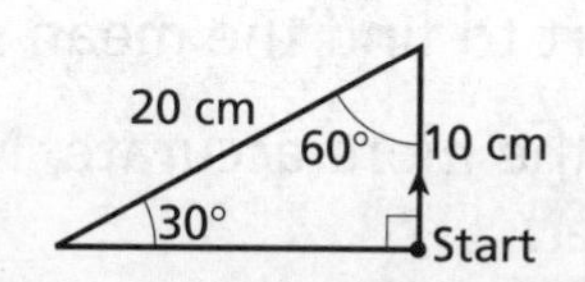

19. When seven dice are rolled together the smallest possible score is 7, that is, by scoring 1 on each dice. What is the largest possible score?
Sixty pupils were divided into six groups: A, B, C, D, E and F.
All of the pupils rolled the seven dice together and their scores were noted.
Nina drew the following bar chart to illustrate the results.

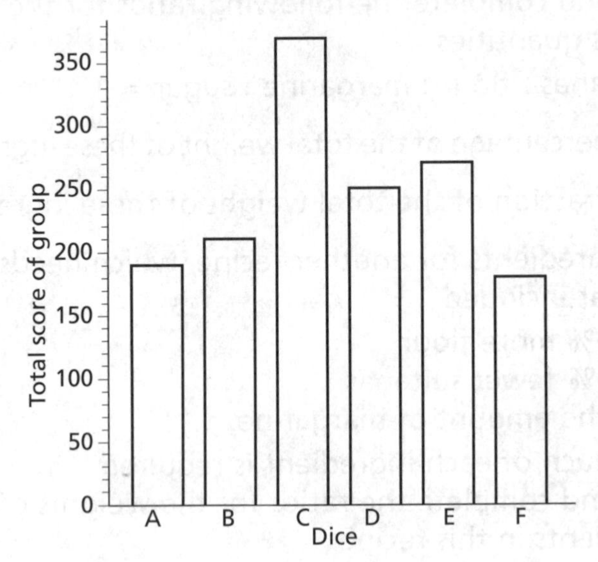

Radeck represented the same information in this bar chart.

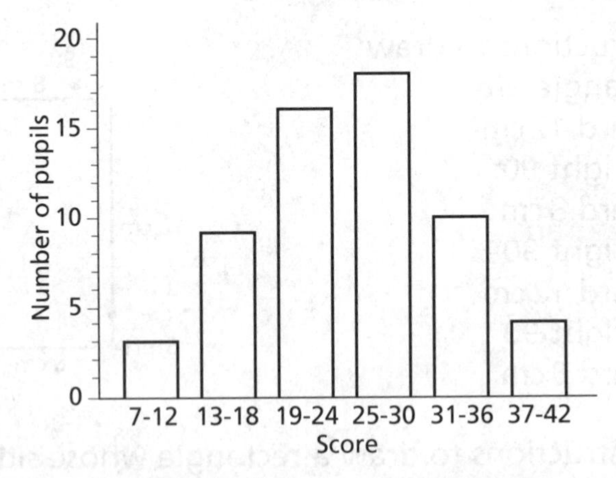

a Nina was asked whether there were more pupils in group A than in group F.
Her possible answers were yes, no or can't say. What is the correct answer?

b Use Nina's bar chart to find the mean score for the 60 pupils.

c Uses Radeck's bar chart to find the mean score for the 60 pupils.

d Whose mean score is the more accurate, Nina's or Radeck's? Give a reason for your answer.

20.

The diameter of the large wheel on a penny farthing bicycle is 54 inches and the diameter of the small wheel is 15 inches.

a How far does the cyclist move forward when the large wheel makes one complete turn?

b If 12 inches = 1 foot, find how many turns the small wheel makes when the bicycle moves forward 40 feet.

c Find the number of turns made by the small wheel for each complete turn of the large wheel.

21. The diagram shows the graph of $y = 2x$.

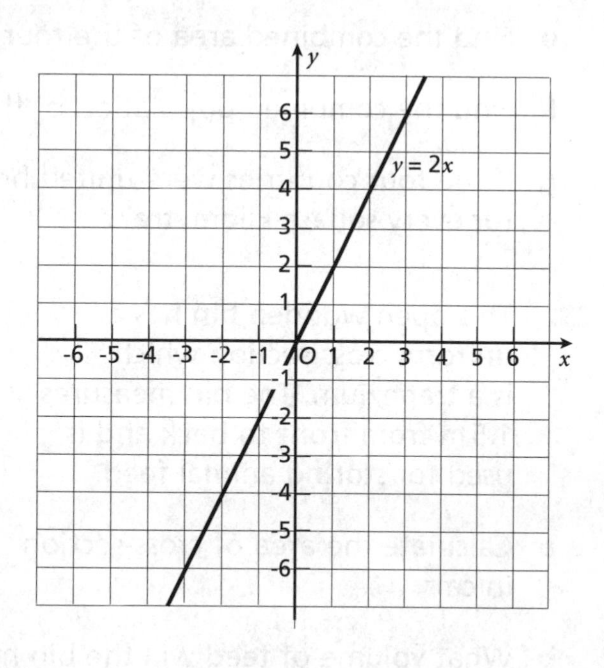

a Copy the diagram onto squared paper. Draw and label the graph of $y = x$.

b Write down the equation of another line that goes through the point (0, 0).

c The straight line with equation $y = 2x - 4$ goes through the point (4, 4). On your own diagram draw the graph of $y = 2x - 4$ and label your line.

d Write down the equation of the straight line that goes through the point (0, −2) and is parallel to the straight line $y = x$.

Level 7 • Questions 22 to 26

22. The table gives information about several European countries.

Country	Population	Area in square kilometres
Ireland	3 514 000	70 284
France	56 400 000	543 965
Finland	4 980 000	338 127
Switzerland	4 710 000	41 293

a Which country has **(i)** the largest area **(ii)** the largest population?

b If all the land in Ireland was shared equally among the population what area would each person get?

c Which country has the most people for each square kilometre?

d Which country has the fewest people for each square kilometre?

e Find the combined area of the four countries in square kilometres.

f Find the combined population of the four countries.

g If the four countries were united how many people would there be for every square kilometre?

23. This open wooden bin has a uniform cross-section which is a trapezium. The bin measures 1.5 m from front to back and is used for storing animal feed.

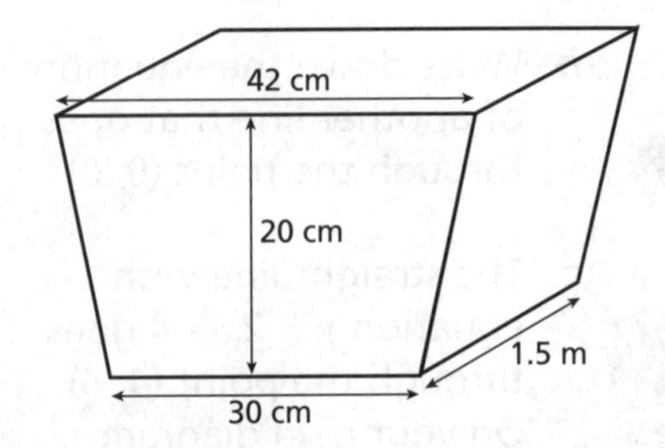

a Calculate the area of cross-section in cm^2.

b What volume of feed will the bin hold when full?

c The feed in the storage bin is used to fill bags which will hold 5 litres. How many bags can be filled completely?

(1 litre – 1000 cm^3)

24a The number, n, of textbooks that Chris can carry must not be more than 15. Write down an inequality to express this fact. Illustrate your inequality on a number line.

b Solve the following inequalities

(i) $x - 7 < 3$ **(ii)** $2x - 5 \leqslant 11$ **(iii)** $6 > 5 - 3x$

c The minimum number of passengers that Summerfield Travel must take to make a profit on a trip to London to see *Phantom of the Opera* is 25. The coach has 47 seats. Which inequality best describes the number, x, of passengers when a profit is made?

A $25 < x < 47$ **B** $25 \leqslant x < 47$ **C** $25 < x \leqslant 47$ **D** $25 \leqslant x \leqslant 47$

d Find the range of values of x for which the inequalities $6 - 4x < 2x - 3 \leqslant 1$ are true.

25a Given that

$$3^2 = 4 \times 3 - 3$$
$$4^2 = 5 \times 4 - 4$$
$$5^2 = 6 \times 5 - 5$$

complete the following formula for n^2 by filling in the blanks.

$$n^2 = (n + 1) \times \square - \square$$

b Find the value of $n^2 + n + 1$ for consecutive whole number values of n from 1 to 10.
How many of these numbers are prime numbers?

c Find, by trying different values, the positive whole number n that satisfies the relation

$$1^3 + 2^3 + 3^3 = (1 + 2 + 3)^n$$

Using this value of n, is it true that

$$1^3 + 2^3 + 3^3 + 4^3 = (1 + 2 + 3 + 4)^n$$

and that $1^3 + 2^3 + 3^3 + 4^3 + 5^3 = (1 + 2 + 3 + 4 + 5)^n$?

26.

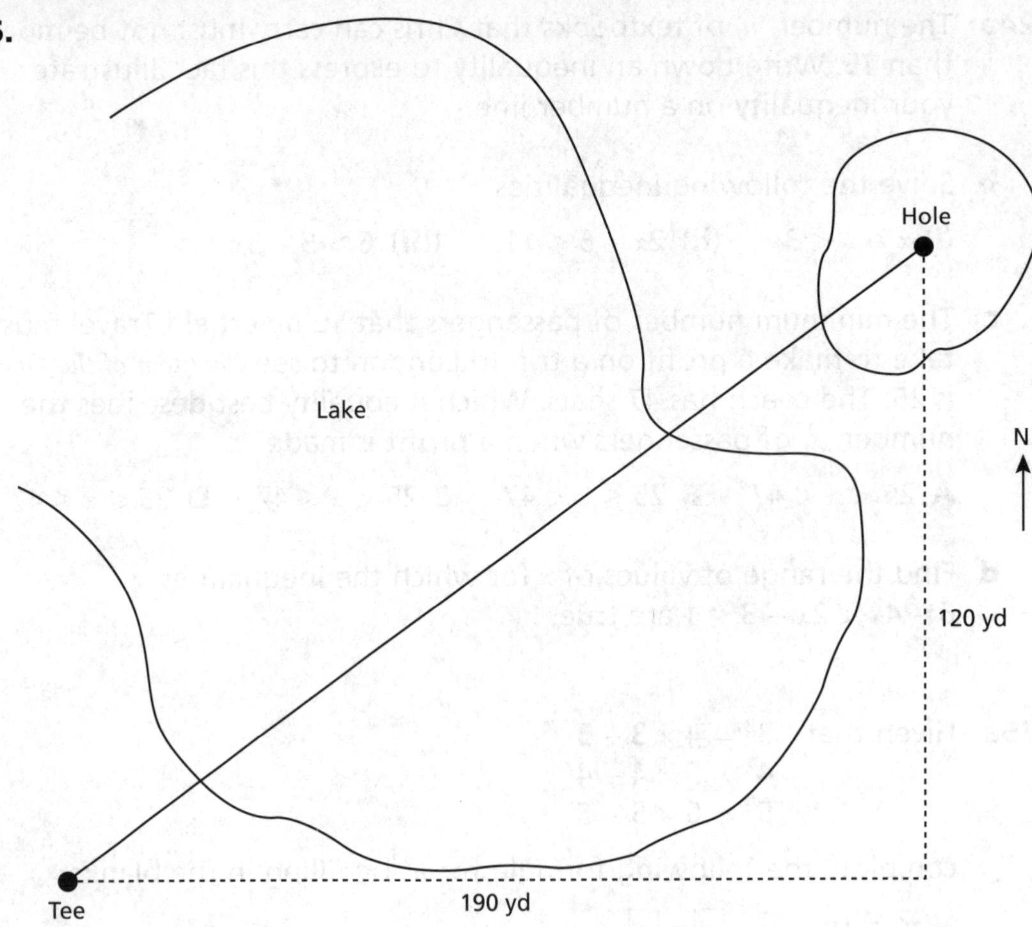

To play the fifth hole at Branfield Golf Course a golfer must hit the ball across a lake.

To walk from the tee to the hole the player has to walk 190 yd due east followed by 120 yd due north.

How far is it in a direct line from the tee to the hole?

27.

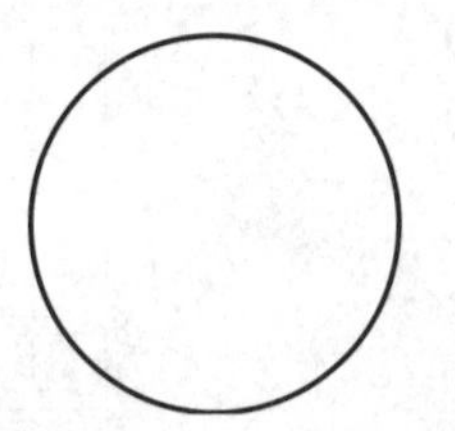

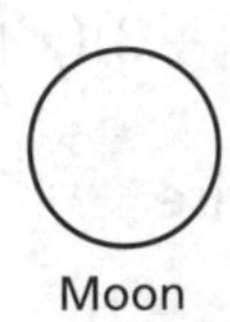

The diameter of the Earth is 12 800 km and its mass is 5.98×10^{24} kg.
The diameter of the Moon is 3500 km and its mass is 7.35×10^{22} kg.

a How many times heavier is the Earth than the Moon?
Give your answer correct to the nearest whole number.

b The volume, V_E, of the Earth is given by the formula

$V_E = 4.2 \times R^3$ where R is the radius of the Earth.

Find the radius of the Earth in **(i)** km **(ii)** m.
Use the formula for V_E to find the volume of the Earth in m^3.

c Find the mass of 1 m^3 of the Earth.

d The volume, V_M, of the Moon is given by

$V_M = 4.2 \times r^3$ where r is the radius of the Moon.

Find the volume of the Moon in m^3.

e Is 1 m^3 of the Earth heavier or lighter than 1 m^3 of the Moon?
Justify your answer.

28. A wedge ABC rests on an inclined plane.
The upper face, AB, of the wedge is horizontal and its side face, BC, is vertical.
A small coin rests on the upper surface of the wedge.

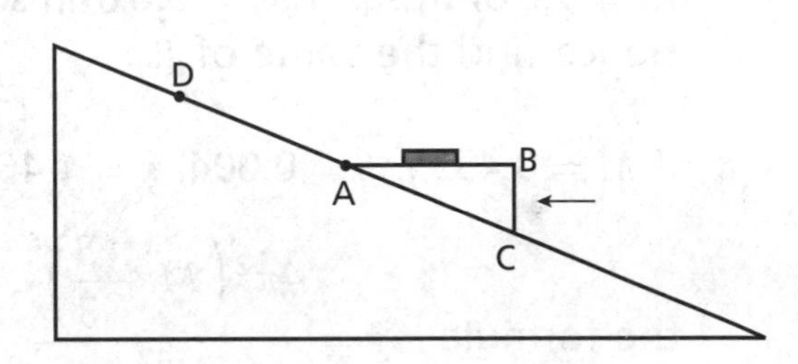

a If AB = 6.3 cm and BC = 2.8 cm find, correct to the nearest tenth of a degree, the inclination of the **plane** to the horizontal.

b The wedge is pushed horizontally so that it slides up the plane. The corner of the wedge, A, moves 8 cm up the plane to D. Find the **vertical** distance through which the coin has risen.

29a Remove the brackets and simplify where possible.

(i) $3(5a+7)$ (iv) $(2x+3)(3x-2)$
(ii) $-2(b-5)$ (v) $(a+3)^2$
(iii) $(y+3)(y+4)$ (vi) $(x-5)(x-2)$

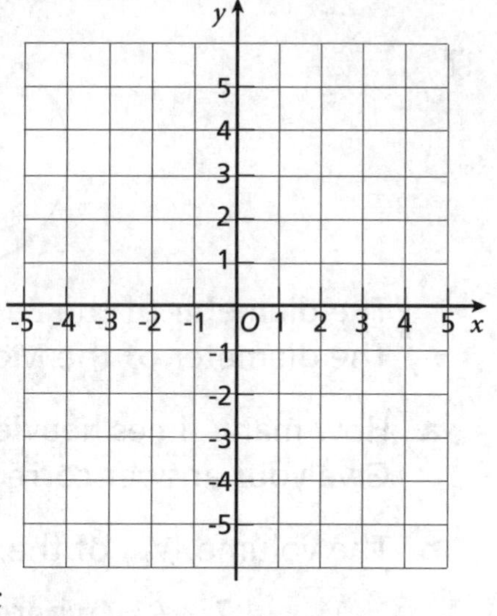

b Factorise

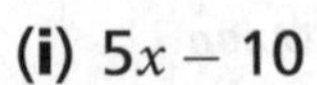

(i) $5x-10$ (iv) x^2-9
(ii) x^3-x^2 (v) $x^2-6x-16$
(iii) $x^2+8x+15$ (vi) $x^2-11x+28$

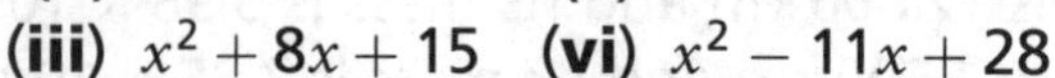

c Solve the equation

(i) $\frac{x}{2}-\frac{1}{4}=\frac{5}{12}$ (iii) $7x-3(x-4)=0$

(ii) $0.25x=3$ (iv) $0.3x=6.5-0.2x$

d Copy the diagram and shade the region defined by the set of inequalities

$x<4,\ y<3,\ x+y\geqslant 0$

30a The total resistance, R ohms, in a circuit which has three resistors in parallel is given by the formula

$$\frac{1}{R}=\frac{1}{R_1}+\frac{1}{R_2}+\frac{1}{R_3}$$

Use this formula to find the value of $\frac{1}{R}$ if $R_1=1.3$ ohms, $R_2=1.6$ ohms and $R_3=0.8$ ohms.
Hence find the value of R.

b If $M=0.4335$, $S=0.004$, $k=1.46$ and $T=1.09$

the formula $g=\frac{4\pi^2\left(M+\frac{S}{3}\right)}{kT^2}$

gives $g=\frac{4\times\pi^2\times\left(0.4335+\frac{0.004}{3}\right)}{1.46\times1.09^2}$

Use a calculator to find the value of g correct to 3 decimal places.

TEST 2 Paper 1

Do not use a calculator for this test.

Level 3 • Questions 1 to 6

1. Eggs are packed in boxes of **6**.

a (i) How many **boxes** does Aziz need to pack **32** eggs?
(ii) How many **more** eggs could be packed?

b Peg has **8 full** boxes of eggs.
How many eggs does she have?

c (i) Sara buys **7** full boxes of eggs.
When she gets them home she finds that **3** are broken.
How many **good** eggs does she have?
(ii) She uses **18** eggs for cooking.
How many boxes does she need for the eggs that **remain**?

2. To answer this question choose the most suitable unit from the following list:

cm hr km minutes g mm seconds kg m mg

Sue wants to telephone the Gas Board but does not have their telephone number.
When she gets to the telephone kiosk she looks it up in 'Yellow Pages'.

What **unit** should she use to measure each of these?
Choose a unit from the above list.

a The **time** it takes to find the telephone number for the Gas Board in the directory.

b The **height** of the telephone kiosk.

c The **thickness** of the 'Yellow Pages' directory.

d The **mass** of the coins she needs to pay for the call.

3. Tino has a supply of **3p** and **5p** stamps.

He wants to send a parcel costing **51p**.

There are three ways of putting on stamps to the correct value.
One way is **2** at **3p** and **9** at **5p.**

Write down the other **two** ways.

Which way uses the **smallest** number of stamps?

4. To go home from school Sonia has to walk a short distance due **north** before she **turns right** to walk along the street in which she lives.

a One day, when Sonia leaves school the wind is blowing **from the north**.
A leaf is being blown along by the wind.
Is the leaf being blown in the **same** direction as Sonia is walking or in the **opposite** direction?

b When Sonia turns into her street George says that she turns through **90° anticlockwise**. Is George correct? Explain your answer.

c When Sonia walks from her home to school does she begin by walking due **east** or due **west**?

d At the end of her street she can

A turn right	**C** turn 90° clockwise
B go straight on	**D** turn 90° anticlockwise

Which one should she choose to continue her journey to school?

5. Each of these shapes has **one** part marked with a **letter** and **another** part marked with a **number**.

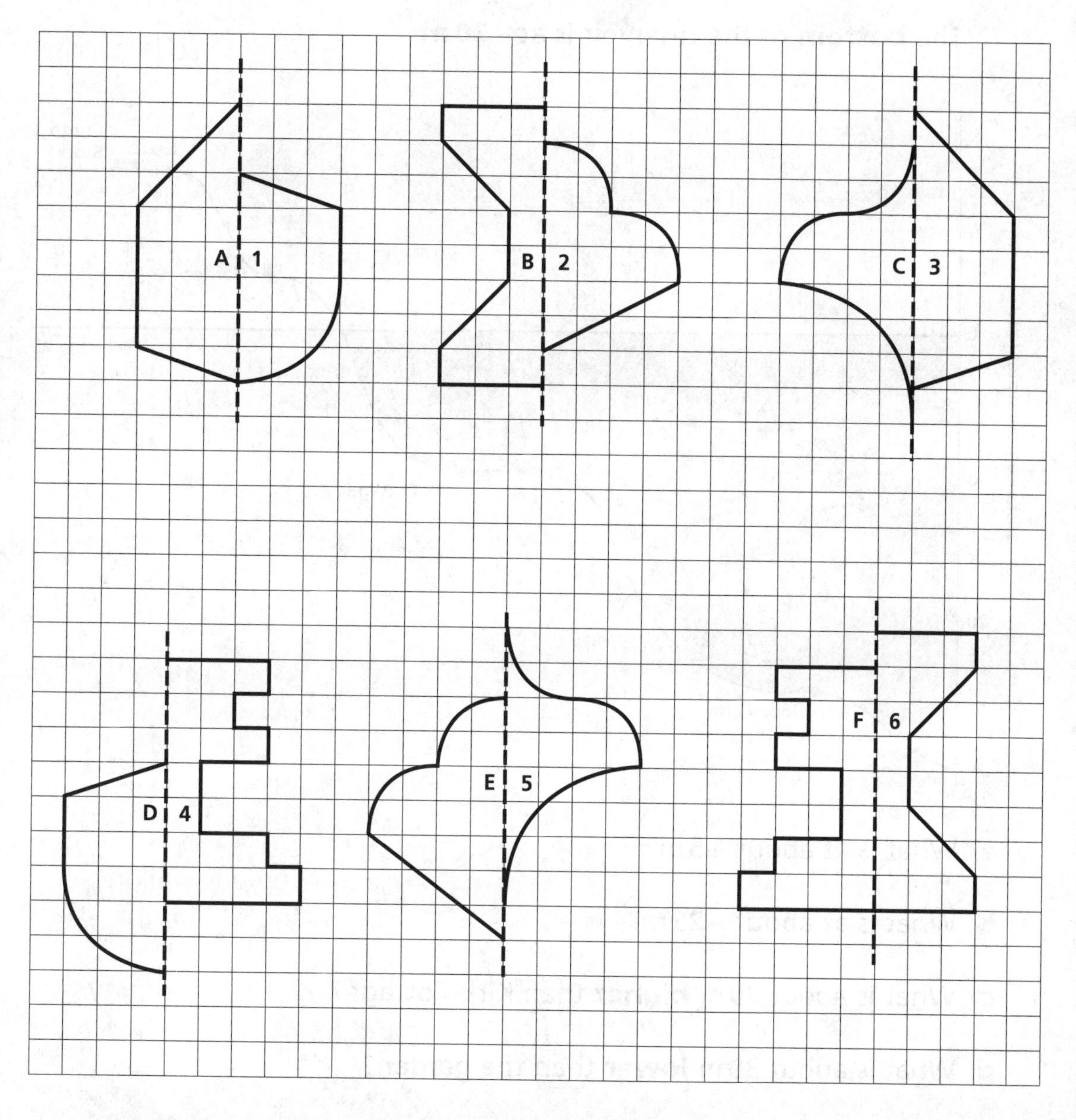

Pair off each **lettered** part with a **numbered** part so that the complete shape has a **line of symmetry.**

For example **A** and **3** make a shape that has a line of symmetry.

6. The picture shows what there is **above** and **below** the water level in a reservoir.

The **bottom** of the reservoir is at $-$**30 m**.

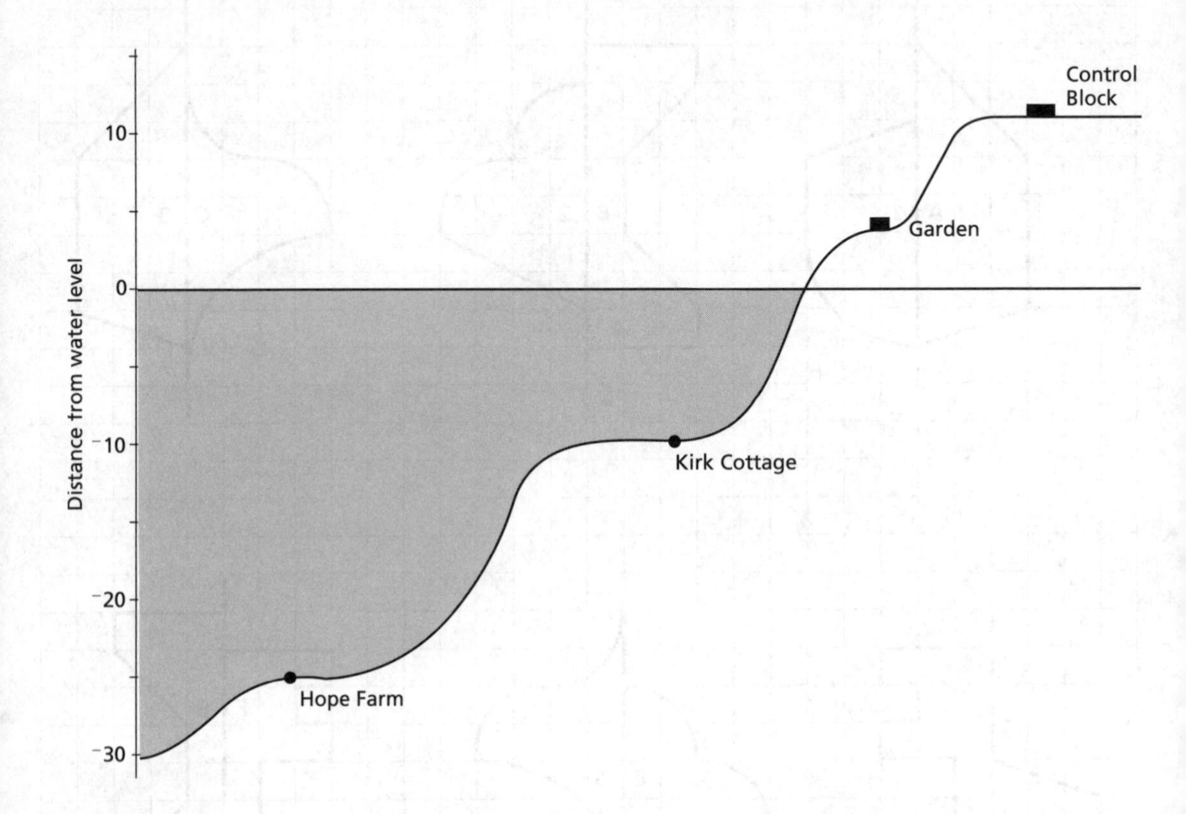

a What is at about +5 m?

b What is at about $-$25 m?

c What is about 20 m **higher** than Kirk Cottage?

d What is about 30 m **lower** than the garden?

7.

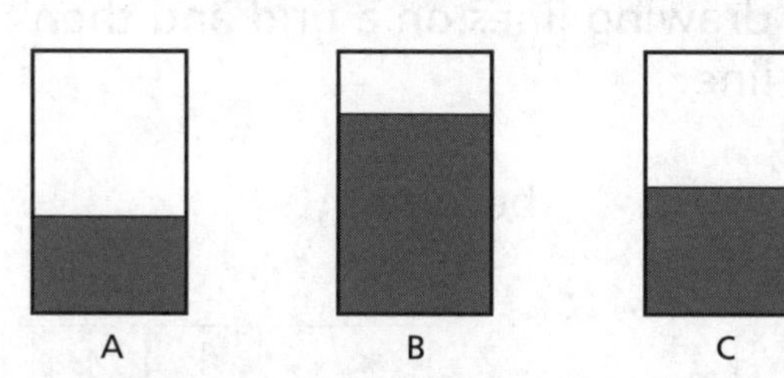

The capacity of each of these cartons is **1** litre.
Choose, from the following list, the correct amount that is in each one.

$\frac{1}{2}$ litre, $\frac{3}{4}$ litre, $\frac{1}{3}$ litre, $\frac{1}{4}$ litre, $\frac{2}{3}$ litre

8. Mr Lewis buys each of his five children an identical stick of Blackpool rock.
The amount that each child has remaining 10 minutes later is shown below.
Colin has eaten about half of his stick.

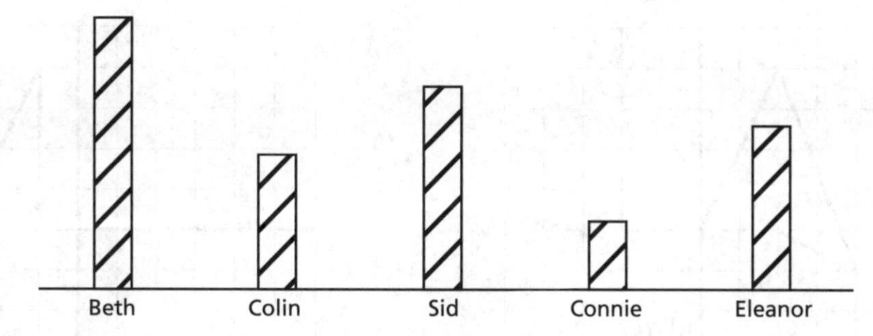

a What fraction does Connie have left?

b What fraction does Sid have left?

Colin has about 50% of his stick left.

c What percentage does Connie have left?

d What percentage has Sid eaten?

e What fraction has Eleanor got left?

f Eventually Beth decides to start her stick. By the time they leave for home she has $\frac{2}{5}$ of it left. Copy the bar that represents Beth's stick and put a **X** where the top of the stick will be when they leave for home.

9. *You may need tracing paper for this question.*

Angi is making patterns by drawing lines on a grid and then reflecting them in a mirror line.

For example becomes

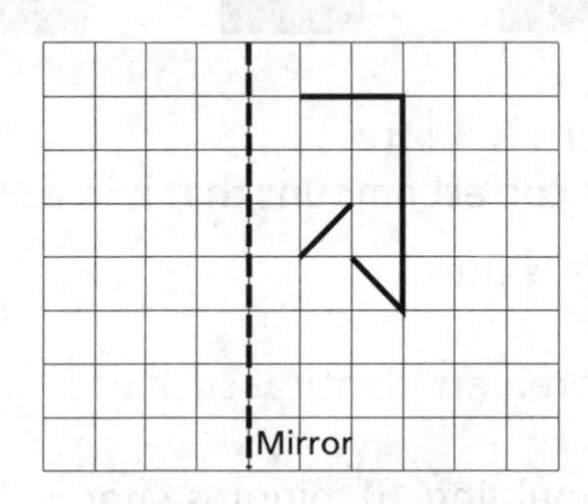

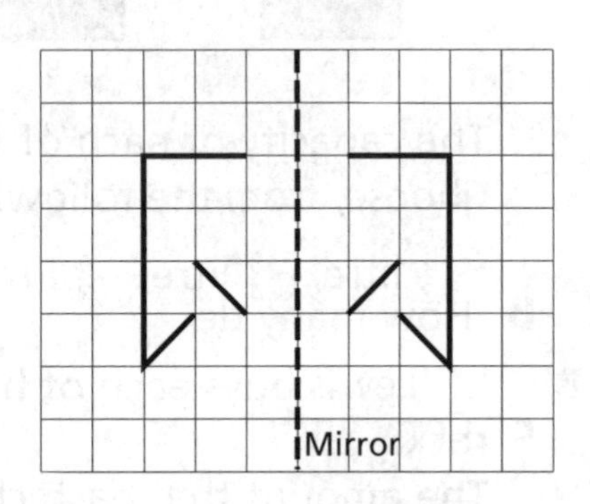

Reflect each group of lines in its mirror line to make a pattern.

a

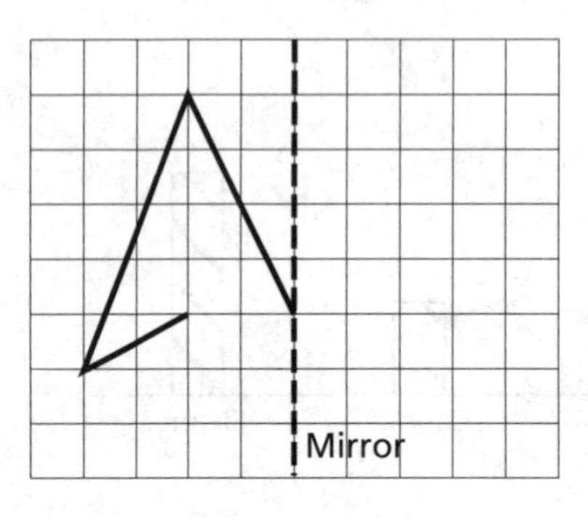

c

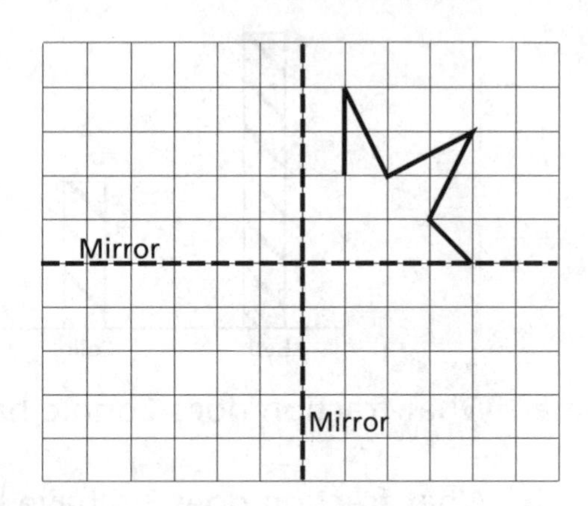

b

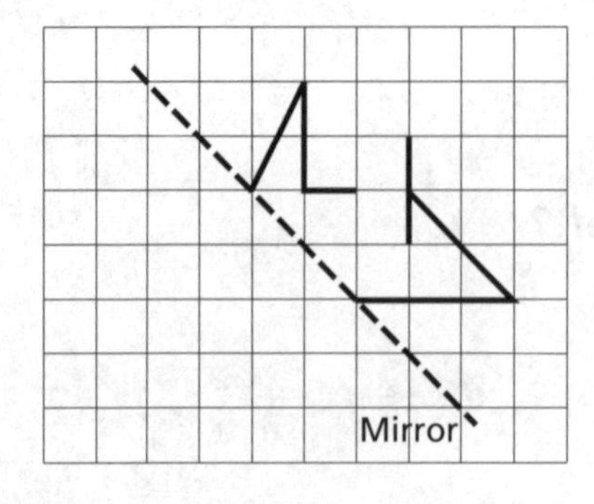

d

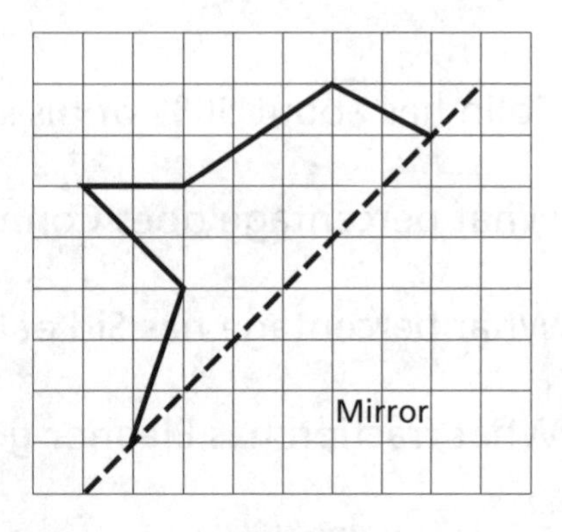

10. Jamie checks a number of packets of paperclips. The number of defective paperclips he found in each packet is listed below.

3	0	1	1	5	3	1	1	1	4
2	5	2	4	1	5	4	0	6	0
4	2	0	1	0	1	3	2	2	

a How many packets did Jamie check?

b How many defective paperclips did he find altogether?

c Copy and complete the following frequency table.

Number of defective paperclips	Tally	Frequency
0		
1		
2		
3		
4		
5		
6		

d Draw a bar chart to show this information and find the mode.

e Find the median number of defective paperclips per packet.

f Jamie checks another packet.
Which is the more likely: that he finds more than 3 defective paperclips or that he finds fewer than 3 defective paperclips?

Level 5 • Questions 11 to 15

11.

Ken is a plumber. He has to work with old pipes, where diameters are measured in imperial units, and modern pipes, where the diameters are measured in metric units.
Ken knows that 1 inch = 25.4 mm.

a What is the diameter, in millimetres, of a $\frac{3}{4}$ inch pipe?

b The diameter of a new plastic pipe is 15 mm. Is this larger or smaller than a $\frac{1}{2}$ inch pipe?

c Ken has to replace an old $1\frac{1}{2}$ inch pipe by a metric pipe that is either exactly the same size or the nearest size above. Which one should he choose: 35 mm, 40 mm, 45 mm or 50 mm?

12. *You need an angle measurer or protractor for this question.*

Jane uses a map to make a sketch of the school grounds.
Her sketch is shown opposite.

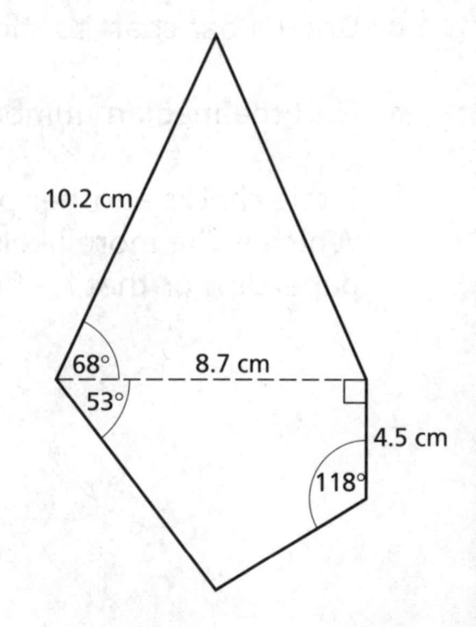

a Make an accurate full-size drawing of the triangle.
Measure and write down the length of the third side.

b Make an accurate full-size drawing of the quadrilateral.
Measure and write down the size of the fourth angle.

13. These patterns are made with matchsticks.

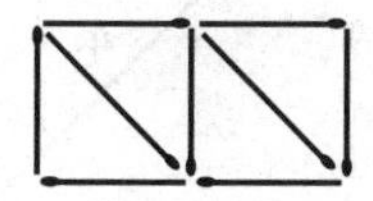

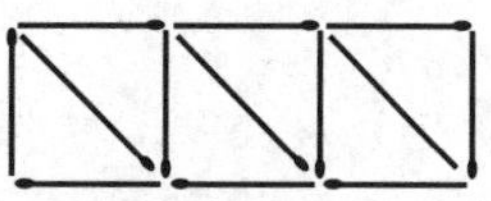

1 square
5 matchsticks

2 squares
9 matchsticks

3 squares
13 matchsticks

Every pattern uses an odd number of matchsticks.
The rule for finding the number of matchsticks in a pattern is

4 times the number of squares plus 1

a Amy wants to make a pattern with 7 squares.
Use the rule to find the number of matchsticks she needs.

b If $M =$ number of matchsticks
and $S =$ number of squares

write down a rule connecting M and S.

c Chris has 40 matchsticks.
What is the largest number of squares he can make in his pattern?
How many matchsticks are left over?

d The rule for finding the number of squares in a pattern is

take 1 away from the number of matchsticks, then divide by 4.

Daryl uses 25 matchsticks.
Use the rule to find how many squares there are in his pattern.

e Sharon uses 49 matchsticks.
Use the rule to find how many squares there are in her pattern.

14.

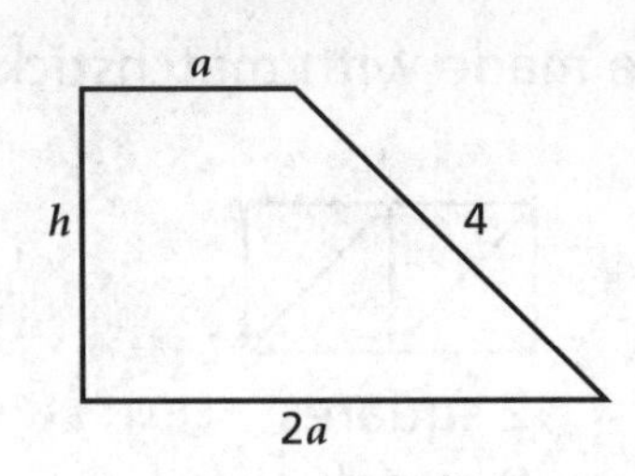

If the perimeter of this shape is p
then $p = 3a + h + 4$

Write an expression, in its simplest form, for the perimeter (p) of each shape.

a

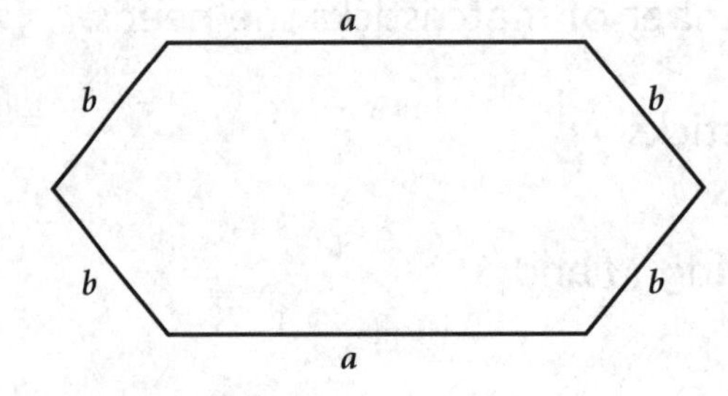

c

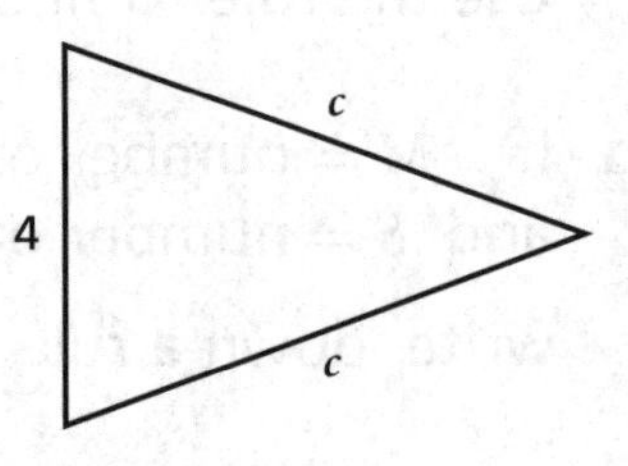

b

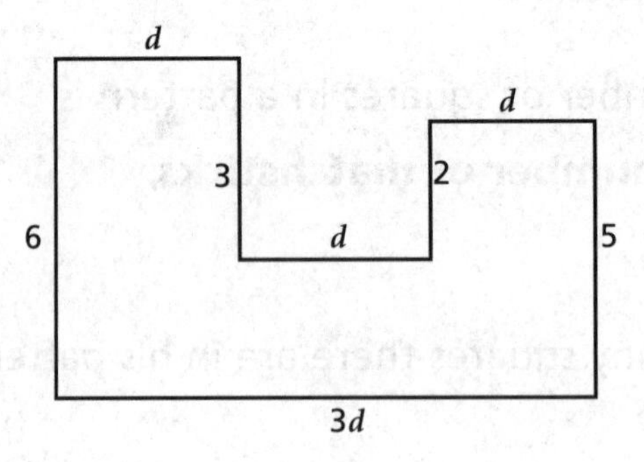

d

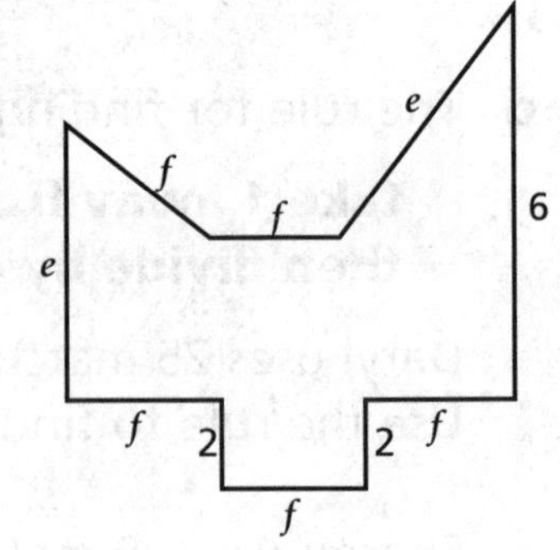

15.

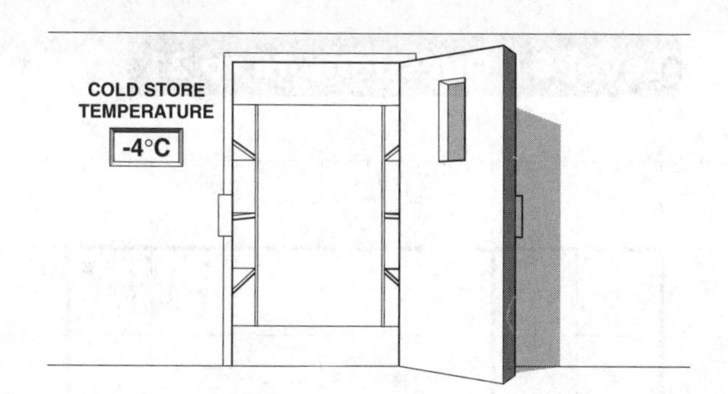

A cold store is to be kept as near as possible to –4°C.
The temperature is recorded every hour.

If the temperature is **above** –4°C it is recorded as a + **number** and

if the temperature is **below** –4°C it is recorded as a – **number**.

For example a temperature of –2°C is recorded as +2
whereas a temperature of –7°C is recorded as –3.

a Copy and complete the following table for a 12-hour period.

Time	6 a.m.	7 a.m.	8 a.m.	9 a.m.	10 a.m.	11 a.m.	12 noon	1 p.m.	2 p.m.	3 p.m.	4 p.m.	5 p.m.	6 p.m.
Actual temperature	–2°C	–7°C	–6°C	–3°C	–2°C	–4°C	–5°C	–8°C	–3°C	–6°C	–5°C	–2°C	0°C
Recorded temperature	+2	–3											

b At 7 a.m. the following day the storekeeper recorded the temperature as –5.
What was the actual temperature?

c By 8 a.m. the temperature had increased by 2°C above the temperature at 7 a.m.
What figure did the storekeeper record?

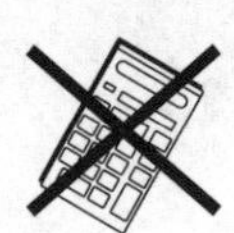

16.

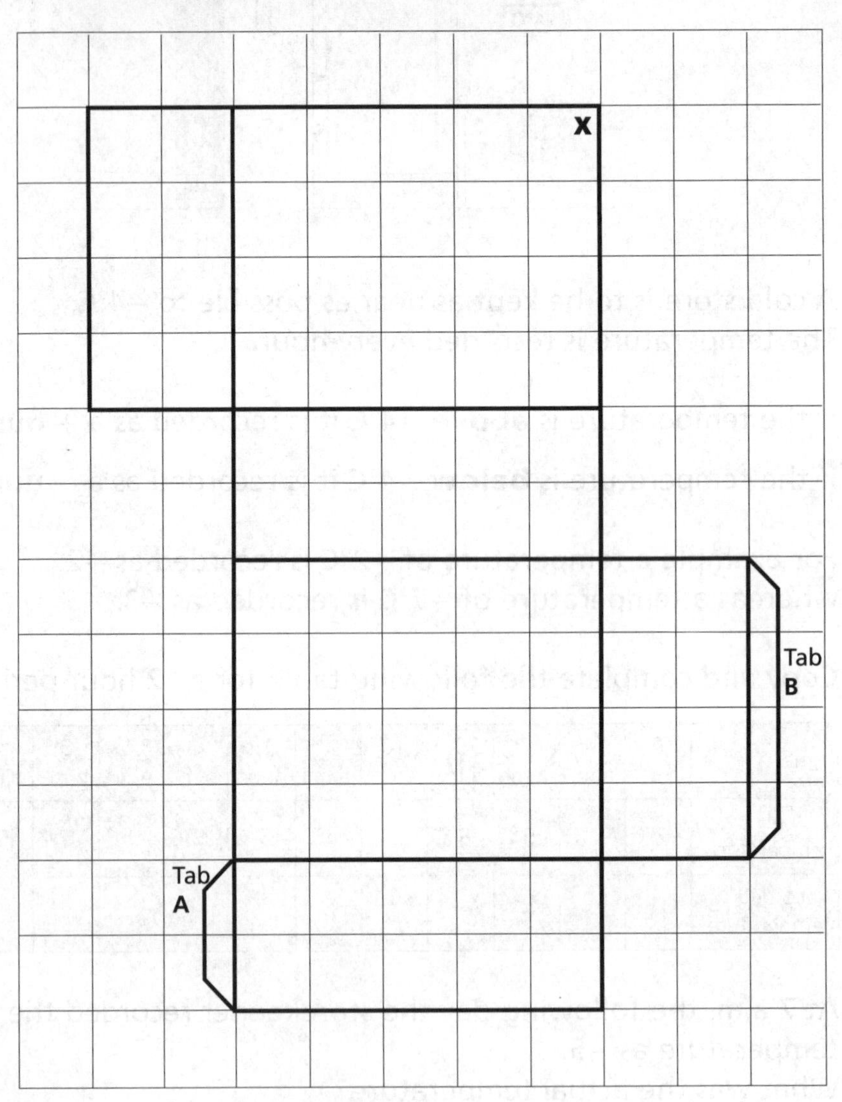

Copy this net onto squared paper.
Draw each square with a side of 1 cm.
This net will fold up to make a cuboid.

a What are the dimensions of the cuboid?

b How many cubes with an edge of 1 cm are needed to fill the same amount of space as this cuboid?

c Write **A** on the edge that Tab **A** will be stuck to.

d Write **B** on the edge that Tab **B** will be stuck to.

e Put **X** in each corner that will meet with the corner marked **X**.

17. Copy the diagram onto squared paper.

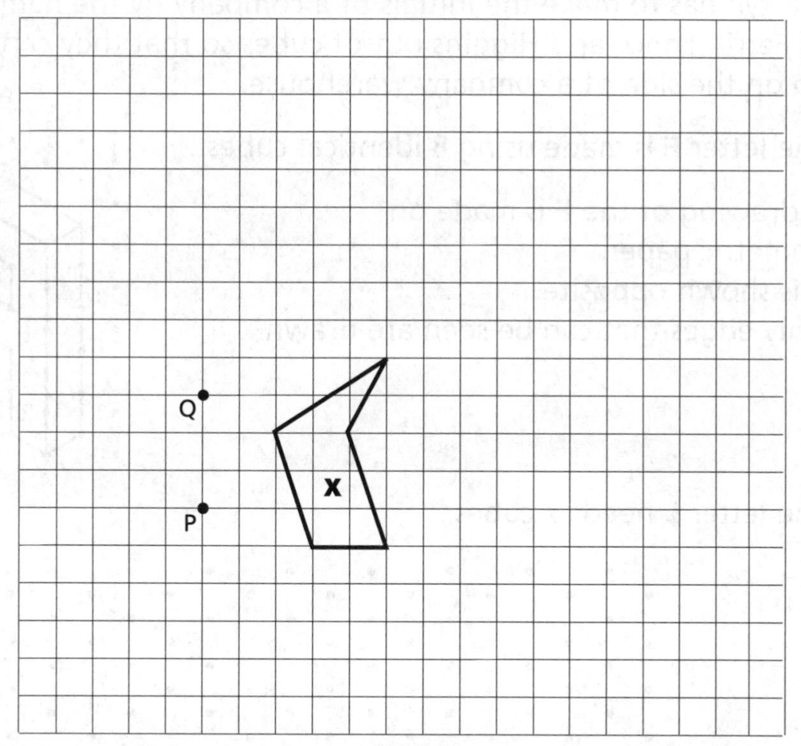

a Draw the image of **X** when it is rotated through 90° clockwise about P. Mark it **A**.

b Draw the image of **X** when it is rotated through 90° anticlockwise about Q. Mark it **B**.

c Draw the image of **X** when it is enlarged by a factor of 3 with P as the centre of enlargement. Mark it **C**.

18a Gail and Rita have £8 between them. Gail has £1.50 more than Rita. How much does Rita have?

b Gail's shopping bag weighs three times as much as Rita's. Together the shopping bags weigh 9.2 kg. How much does Gail's bag weigh?

c At the Leisure Centre Gail and Rita hired the running machine between them for $\frac{1}{2}$ hour. They took turns on it. If Rita could have stayed on the running machine for an extra 3 minutes after the $\frac{1}{2}$ hour was up, she would have spent twice as long on it as Gail. How long was Rita on the running machine?

19. *You need isometric graph paper for this question.*

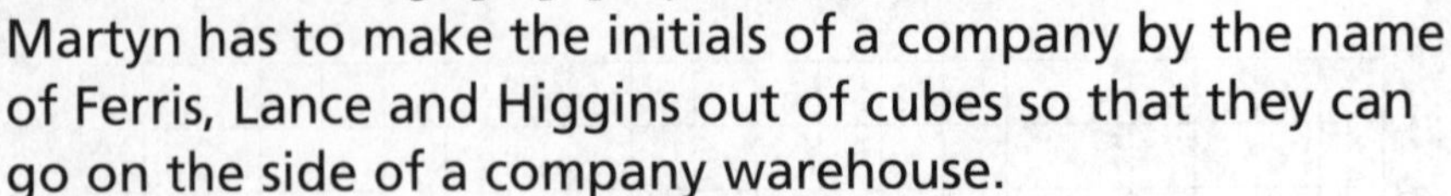

Martyn has to make the initials of a company by the name of Ferris, Lance and Higgins out of cubes so that they can go on the side of a company warehouse.

The letter **F** is made using 8 identical cubes.

A drawing of the **F** is made on isometric paper.
It is shown opposite.
Only edges that can be seen are drawn.

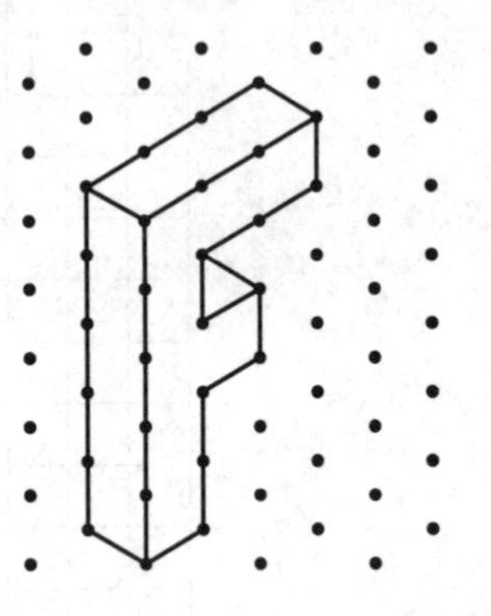

The letter **L** needs 7 cubes.

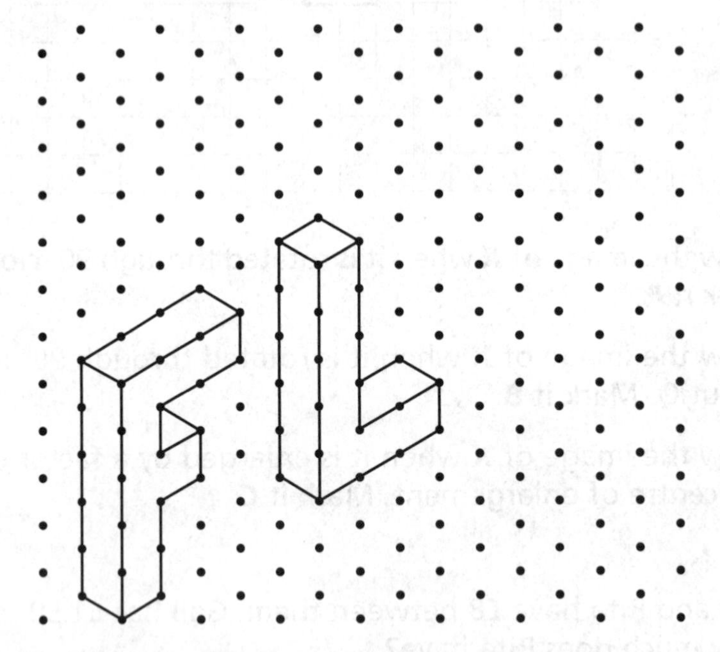

a Copy the letters **F** and **L** onto isometric graph paper and add the letter **H** so that the width and height of the **H** is equal to that of the **F** and the **L**.
How many cubes are needed to make the **H**?

Draw on your graph paper

b the letter **F** when it is turned on its back

c the letter **L** when it is turned upside down

d the letter **H** when it is turned on its side.

20.

Gary's newsagent sells ballpoint pens. She also sells pencils.
A pen costs 70 p and a pencil costs 50 p.

The cost, C pence, of buying x pens and y pencils can be calculated from the formula

$$C = 70x + 50y$$

a Gary bought 6 pens and 4 pencils.
Work out the cost.

b Lila spent £6.40 when she bought some pens and some pencils.
How many pence did Lila spend?
She bought 7 pens. How many pencils did she buy?

c By the end of the first quarter of last year the sales of pens and pencils totalled 450, of which 252 were pens.
What percentage of the total sold were **(i)** pens **(ii)** pencils?

d For the whole of the year the newsagent sold 1767 pens and pencils altogether.
Next year she estimates that she will sell about the same number, but that the sale of pens to pencils will be in the ratio 2 : 1.

The cost of a pen will increase to 75 p but the cost of a pencil will remain at 50 p.

Estimate **(i)** the number of pens she hopes to sell
(ii) the number of pencils she hopes to sell
(iii) the amount of money she will take for the year from the sale of pens and pencils.

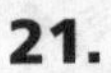

21.

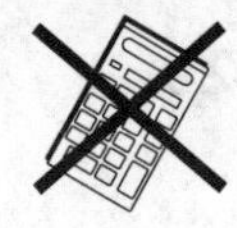

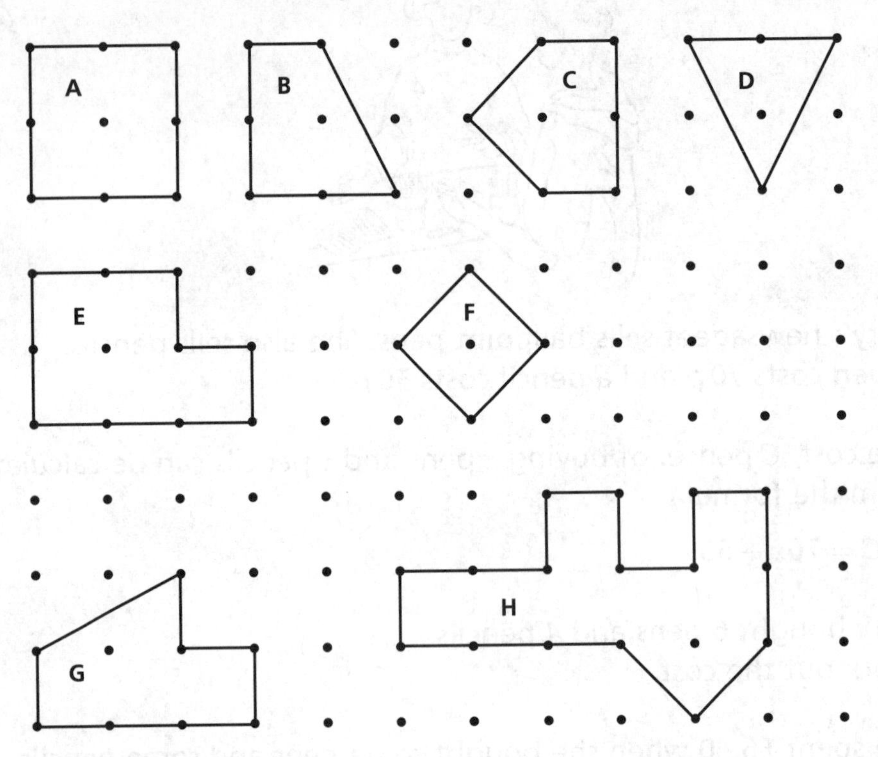

The shapes are drawn on a 1 centimetre grid.

Each polygon surrounds one grid intersection that is marked with a dot.

a Copy and complete this table which shows the number of dots on the boundary of each shape and its area.

Shape	Number of dots on boundary	Area in cm^2
A	8	4
B		
C		
D		

b On your own grid draw some more polygons that surround one dot and add the information you get from them to your table.

c Find a formula connecting A, the area of the shape in square centimetres, and the number, n, of dots on its boundary.

d What is the area of a polygon with one dot inside and 12 dots on its boundary?

e How many dots are there on the boundary of a polygon with an area of seven square centimetres if there is one dot inside?

22.

The Music department wishes to transport 162 Year 11 pupils plus 16 teachers, to London, which is 90 miles away, to attend a promenade concert at the Albert Hall. The local bus company has two kinds of coaches, 29-seaters and 42-seaters. Fuel consumption is 15 miles per gallon for a small coach and 12 miles per gallon for a large one. Fuel costs £2.50 per gallon and the overheads, including the driver, amount to £100 per coach.

a How many gallons of fuel are used for this trip by **(i)** a 29-seater **(ii)** a 42-seater?

b Find, for each size of coach, the combined cost of fuel and overheads for this journey.

c How many 29-seater coaches would be needed if it was decided to use two 42-seaters?

d What combination of coaches provides the cheapest way of hiring coaches for this school trip?
How much does this work out per pupil if the teachers travel free?
Give your answer correct to the nearest 5 p, rounded upwards.

23a Solve the inequalities
(i) $x - 8 \leqslant -5$ **(ii)** $4x - 3 > 9$

b Find the range of values of x for which the pair of inequalities
$5x + 1 \geqslant 3$ and $4x - 3 < 4$ are true.
Illustrate your answer on a number line.

c **(i)** Write down the next two terms in the sequence 3, 6, 11, 18,
(ii) Find a formula for the nth term in terms of n.
(iii) Use your formula to find the value of n that gives an nth term of 102.

24a Copy the diagram onto squared paper.
Which of the equations $x + y = 5$ and $3y = x + 9$ is the equation of the straight line drawn on the graph?

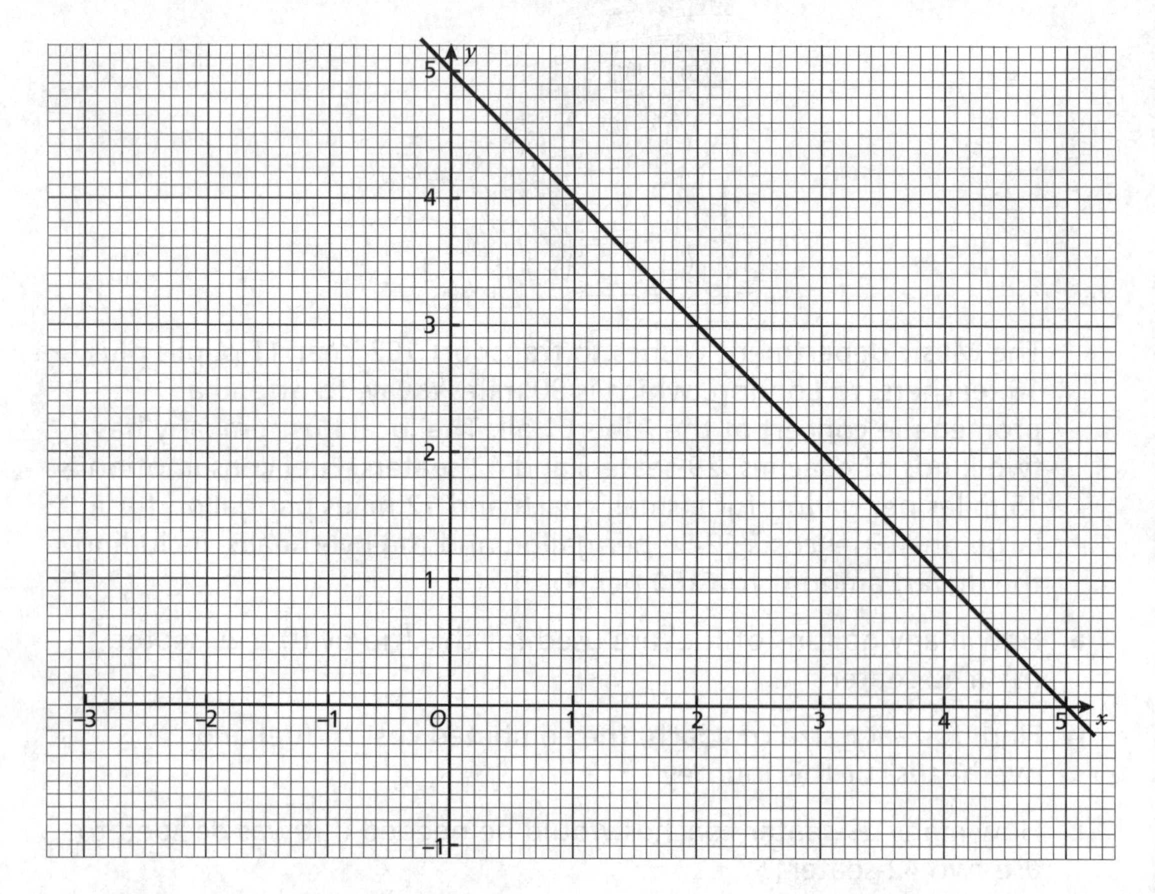

b Write down the coordinates of three points on this line.

c For the other equation find the values of y that correspond to the values of x given in the table.

x	−3	0	3
y			

d Plot these points on your graph and draw the straight line through them.

e Use your graph to solve the simultaneous equations

$$x + y = 5$$
$$3y = x + 9$$

f Solve, without using a graph, the simultaneous equations

$$x + y = 5$$
$$x - 3y = -9$$

25a A wheel of radius 15 cm rolls down a garden path which is inclined at 20° to the horizontal. Sketch the locus of the centre of the wheel.

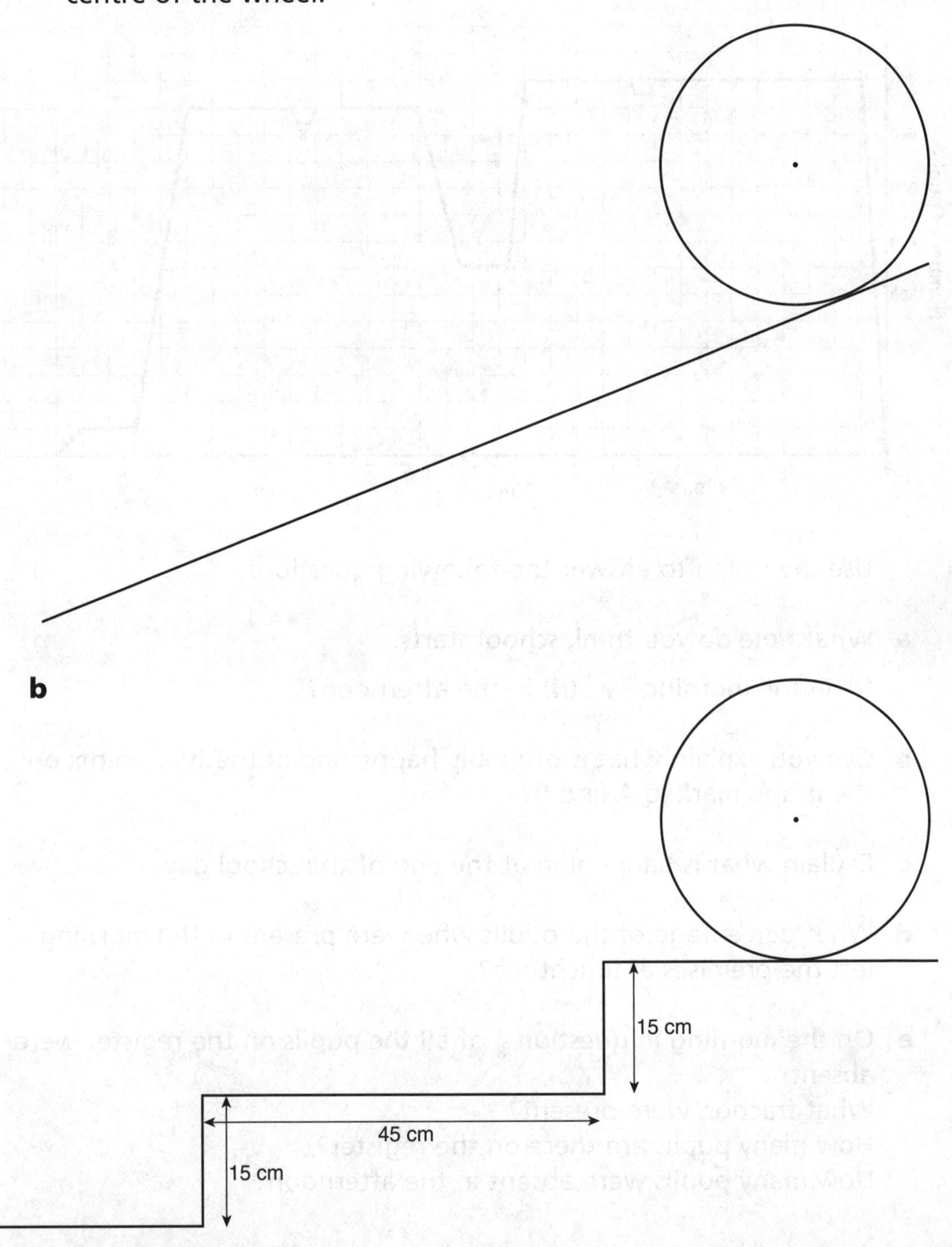

In another part of the garden the wheel rolls down two steps, each 15 cm deep, which are 45 cm apart. Sketch the locus of the centre of the wheel.

26. The graph shows the number of pupils on the premises at St Joseph's Comprehensive School one day last term.

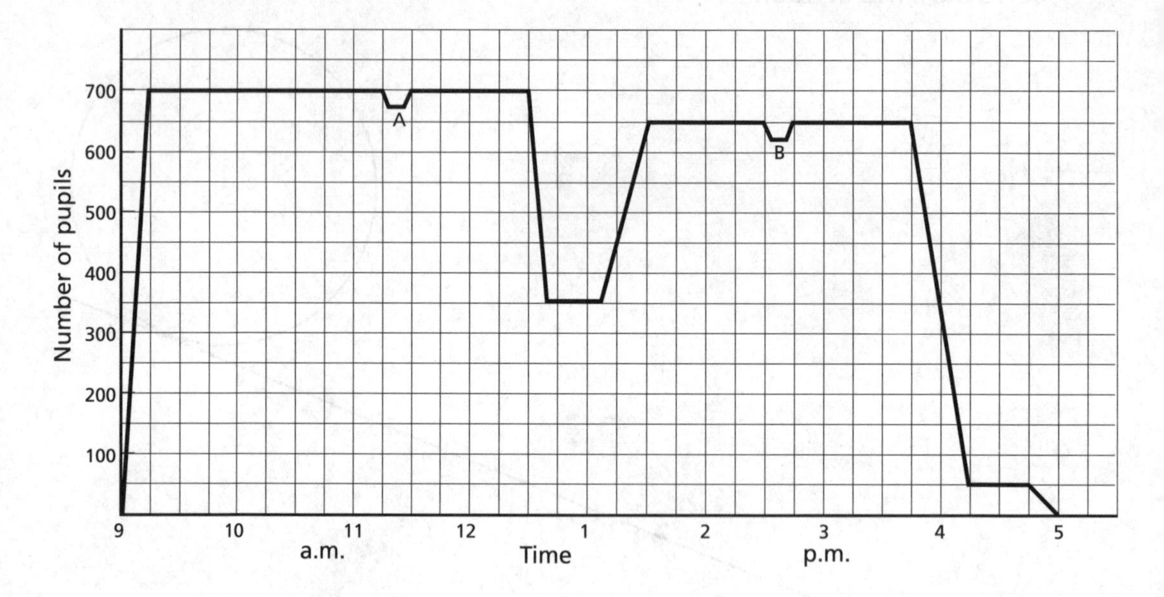

Use the graph to answer the following questions.

a What time do you think school starts:

(i) in the morning **(ii)** in the afternoon?

b Can you explain what is probably happening at the two points on the graph marked A and B?

c Explain what is happening at the end of the school day.

d What percentage of the pupils who were present in the morning left the premises at lunchtime?

e On the morning in question $\frac{1}{8}$ of all the pupils on the register were absent.
What fraction were present?
How many pupils are there on the register?
How many pupils were absent in the afternoon?

27. In real life situations there are times when we do not have enough information to solve a problem. On other occasions we have more than enough. If there is too much we use what is relevant and discard the rest.
Answer each question by making use of the relevant information.

a Yvonne is watching a programme on television. What time should it finish?

Additional information:

(i) The programme lasts 40 minutes.
(ii) It is one of TV's most popular programmes.
(iii) She started watching it when it started at 7.30 p.m.
(iv) It is about two-thirds of the way through at the moment.

b Cyril is at home and is due to attend a meeting of the Motor Club at 7.00 p.m. It will take him 20 minutes to walk there. Will he probably be late?

Additional information:

(i) His car has broken down so he must walk.
(ii) His watch is 10 minutes fast.
(iii) He had finished his meal by 6.30 p.m. by his watch.
(iv) It is 6.45 p.m. by his watch now.

c Mrs Buck makes dresses for people who bring her the material. How much profit did she make last week?

Additional information:

(i) She charges £4.50 per hour.
(ii) She works about forty hours each week.
(iii) She never works on a Sunday.
(iv) Her expenses come to about £10 a week.
(v) She usually starts work at 9.30 a.m.

28.

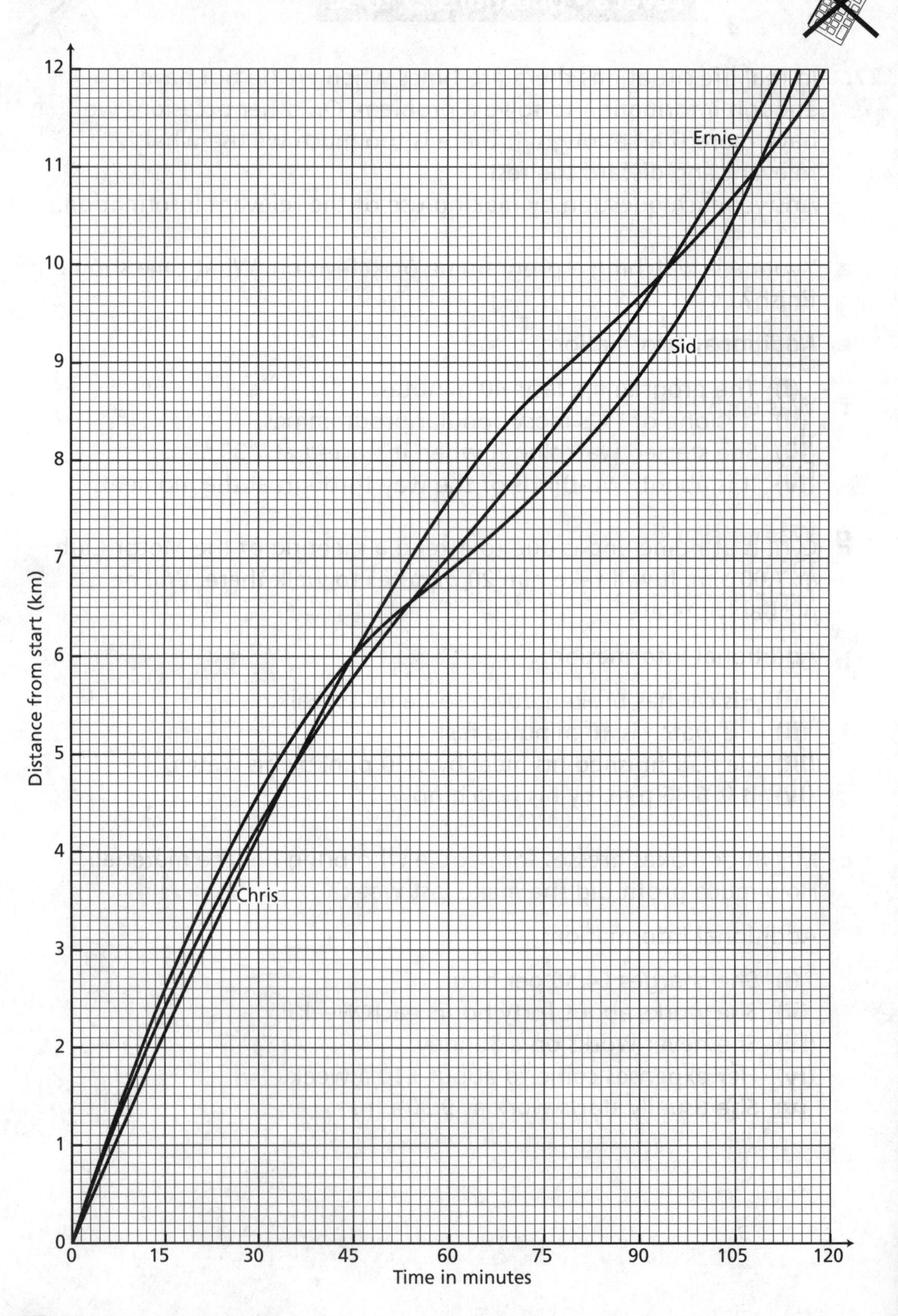

Distance from start (km)
12
11
10
9
8
7
6
5
4
3
2
1
0
Ernie
Sid
Chris
0
15
30
45
60
75
90
105
120
Time in minutes

The graph shows the journeys of Chris, Ernie and Sid in a sponsored walk.

a How long was the walk?

b How long did Chris take?

c Who was the fastest walker at the beginning of the walk?

d Which of the three was the first to finish?

e How many times did Chris pass Sid?

f Was each of the three in front of the other two at some stage of the race?
Explain your answer.

g Was each of the three behind the other two at some time during the race?
Explain your answer.

h Over which part of the course was the going easiest?

i Which of the three was in front of the other two for the longest time?
About how long was this?

29a Milo often goes to see his local football team when they play at home. The probability that he goes on foot is $\frac{1}{2}$, by car is $\frac{1}{6}$ or on the bus is $\frac{1}{3}$.
What is the probability that he goes

(i) on foot or by car **(ii)** by car or on the bus?

b Two dice are rolled. What is the probability of getting a double 6?

c A school committee consists of 7 boys and 5 girls. Of the boys, 3 have blue eyes and the rest do not, and of the girls, 2 have blue eyes and the rest do not. One boy and one girl are chosen at random to represent the committee at a conference. What is the probability that

(i) both pupils have blue eyes
(ii) one pupil has blue eyes and one pupil does not?

30a Ken and Wyn were doing some practical work to find the volume of a lump of metal. Ken said the volume was 54 cm^2 but Wyn insisted that it was 54 cm^3. Who was definitely wrong?
Explain your answer.

b What units would you use to measure the surface area of a sphere if the radius is given in centimetres?

c Two lengths are given as p cm and q cm. Does each expression represent a length, an area, a volume, or none of these?

A $\frac{p^2 - q^2}{2p}$ **B** $p^2q + q^2p$ **C** $3p(q - 4)$ **D** $(p + q)(p - q)$

d A model is a cm long, b cm wide and c cm tall.
Which of the following expressions could give its total surface area?

A $3a^2b + b^2c$ **B** $2ab + 5abc$ **C** $5(a + b)(2a - c)$ **D** $\frac{3ab}{c} + bc$

TEST 2 Paper 2

Calculators may be used for this test.

Level 3 • Questions 1 to 6

1. The caretaker is arranging **36** chairs so that Mrs Dunster can meet the parents of the pupils in her class. He can arrange the chairs to form a square of **6 rows** with **6 chairs** in each row.

a Draw a diagram to show that the chairs can be arranged in **2** rows with the **same** number of chairs in each row.

b Copy and complete the table to show **all the different ways** in which the caretaker can arrange the chairs in rows with the **same** number of chairs in **every** row.

Number of rows	Number of chairs in each row
1	36
2	
6	6
18	1
36	1

c On another occasion the caretaker has to lay out **48** chairs.
Can these chairs be arranged so that the number of chairs in each row is **(i) 7** **(ii) 8**?
Justify your answer.

2. Five players took part in a darts competition.
The winner was the player who scored most in **one turn** of three darts.

Their scores are given in the table.

	1st turn	2nd turn	3rd turn	4th turn
George	64	82	63	72
Mavis	43	66	54	20
Phil	26	34	37	53
Lyn	41	64	42	18
Peter	72	74	98	23

a How many did **Lyn** score on her **third** turn?

b How many did **Phil** score on his **second** turn?

c Who was in the lead after **two** turns?

d Who always scored **more** than Lyn?

e Who got better **every** turn?

f Who **won** the competition?

Suppose the competition had been to get the highest total score after four turns.

g Who would have **won**?

h Is this the **same** person who won under the **agreed** rules?

i Who would have been leading after **three** turns?

j Who would have been **last**?

3.

One week last summer four voluntary workers spent their lunch breaks collecting money for charity outside the four entrances to the local supermarket.
The supermarket is part of a large shopping centre.
The amounts, in pounds, each person collected are shown in the table.

	Mon	Tues	Wed	Thurs	Fri
Andrea	7.22	7.30	5.20	8.84	9.10
Ben	3.50	3.20	2.25	3.70	3.80
Cynthia	8.30	8.42	4.30	9.15	10.20
Darryl	6.50	6.77	3.94	8.67	9.50

a How much did **each** person collect in the week?

b How much was collected **each day**?

c Give a possible reason why the amount **Ben** collected was much **less** than each of the others.

d Why do you think the total amount collected was **less** on **Wednesday** than on any other day?

e How much was collected **altogether**?

f How much was collected altogether **correct to the nearest £10**?

4.

The timetable for the first three buses from Penford to Wade on a weekday is given below.

Penford	*depart*	09.45	11.25	12.15
Royston	*arrive*	10.00	11.40	12.30
	depart	10.05	11.45	12.35
Wade	*arrive*	10.40	12.20	13.10

a Helen catches the 11.25 bus from Penford.
What time does she arrive at **(i) Royston** **(ii) Wade**?

b How many **minutes** does Helen's journey take from **Penford** to

(i) Royston (ii) Wade?

c Gary lives in **Royston**.
It took him **10** minutes to walk to the bus stop and he waited **5** minutes before the bus arrived.
What time did Gary leave home if he caught the **10.05** bus from **Royston** to **Wade**?

Janet is **10** minutes **late** getting to the bus stop in Penford to catch the **11.25** bus to Wade.

d How **long** does she have to **wait** for the next bus?

e What time should she arrive in **Wade**?

f Linda wants to catch the **12.15** from **Penford** at **Royston** to go to see her brother who lives in Wade. She takes **7** minutes to walk to the bus stop.
What is the **latest** she can leave home to be at the bus stop in time?

5. Angela has **20** square tiles.

She arranges **18** of them in a pattern as shown opposite.

Copy this shape **twice** onto squared paper.

A

a Does this shape have **line** symmetry about a mirror line passing through **A**?

If it does draw the line of symmetry.

If it does not, add the other 2 tiles so that the resulting shape has a line of symmetry.
Draw the mirror line.

b Does this shape have **rotational** symmetry?

If it does mark the centre of rotation **X**.

If it does not, add the other 2 tiles so that the resulting shape has rotational symmetry.
Mark the centre of rotation with an **X**.

6a When full, which of these vessels could hold about $\frac{3}{4}$ litre?

A a teacup **B** a bucket **C** an egg cup **D** a jug

b The weight of a newly born baby could be about

A 30 kg **B** 3 kg **C** 3 g **D** 30 mg?

c The length of a family car could be about

A 4 cm **B** 4 km **C** 4 m **D** 40 mm?

d The area of a football field could be about

A 10 000 mm^2 **B** 4000 cm^2 **C** 10 000 m^2 **D** 3 km^2?

7. This triangle is drawn accurately.
The length of the longest side is 9.5 cm.

a Tim says that the perimeter of the triangle is about 18 cm.
Without measuring explain why Tim must be wrong.

b Measure, correct to 0.1 of a centimetre, the lengths of the other two sides.

c Add up the lengths of the three sides of the triangle to find its perimeter.

8. Alan has a pile of cubes, all with an edge of 1 cm.
He places 2 cubes side by side on the table.
The total surface area of the resulting shape that can be seen is 8 cm^2.

a What surface area can be seen if he puts 3 cubes side by side in a row?
What surface area can be seen if he puts 4 cubes side by side in a row?
Copy and complete the following table.

Number of cubes in the row	2	3	4	5	6	7	8
Surface area that can be seen in cm^2	8						

b Alan arranges 8 cubes on the table to make one large cube.
What is the length of an edge of this cube?
What surface area is visible for this cube?

c Sheila says that the 8 cubes can be arranged on the table as a single shape so that the total surface area of the shape that can be seen is less than when they are arranged as the large cube.
Explain why Sheila is wrong.

9.

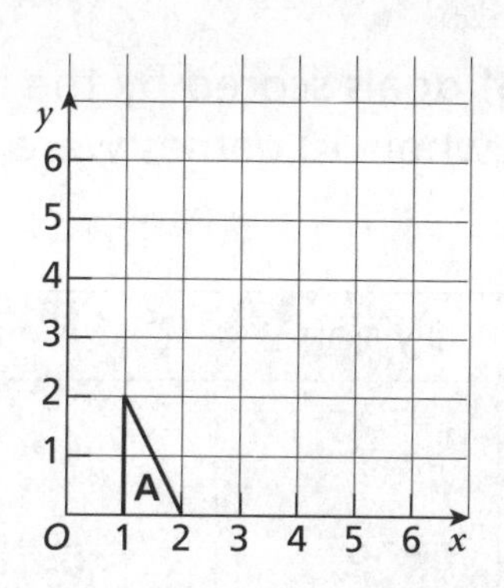

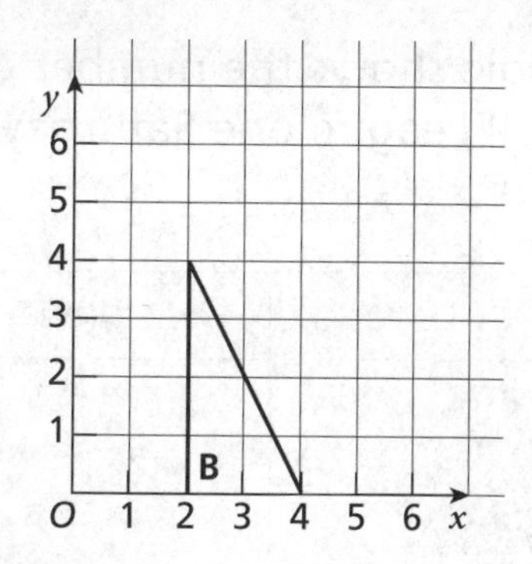

The coordinates of the three corners of triangle **A** are (1, 0), (2, 0) and (1, 2).
The area of triangle **A** is 1 square unit.
The coordinates of the three corners of another triangle **B** are found by multiplying the coordinates of triangle **A** by 2.

Coordinates of the corners of triangle **A**	Coordinates of the corners of triangle **B**
(1, 0) (2, 0) (1, 2)	(2, 0) (4, 0) (2, 4)

a Find the area of triangle **B** in square units.

b The coordinates of the corners of triangle **C** are found by multiplying every coordinate of the corners of triangle **A** by 3.
Copy and complete this table.

Coordinates of the corners of triangle **A**	Coordinates of the corners of triangle **C**
(1, 0) (2, 0) (1, 2)	

Plot these points on a grid and join them to give triangle **C**.

What is the area of triangle **C**?

c Azim multiplies all the coordinates of triangle **A** by another number.
Two of the points have coordinates (5, 0) and (10, 0).
What are the coordinates of the third corner of this triangle?
What is the area of this triangle?

10. The table shows the number of goals scored by the home side in the Football League one Saturday when 10 games were played in each division

Premier League	Division 1	Division 2	Division 3
0	2	1	2
2	0	3	2
1	1	2	0
1	3	0	3
0	2	2	3
2	1	3	2
1	2	1	4
1	1	4	3
1	2	2	0
2	3	3	2

a Quentin says that the mode for the Premier League matches is 1. Explain why Quentin in right.

b What is the mode for the Division 3 matches?

c Copy and complete the following tally chart for each division.

Goals	Tally				Total goals for all 4 divisions
	Premier League	Division 1	Division 2	Division 3	
0 1 2 3 4					

Look at the tally marks in your chart.
What do you notice about the number of goals scored by the home sides in the different divisions?

11. Three of these shapes have rotational symmetry.

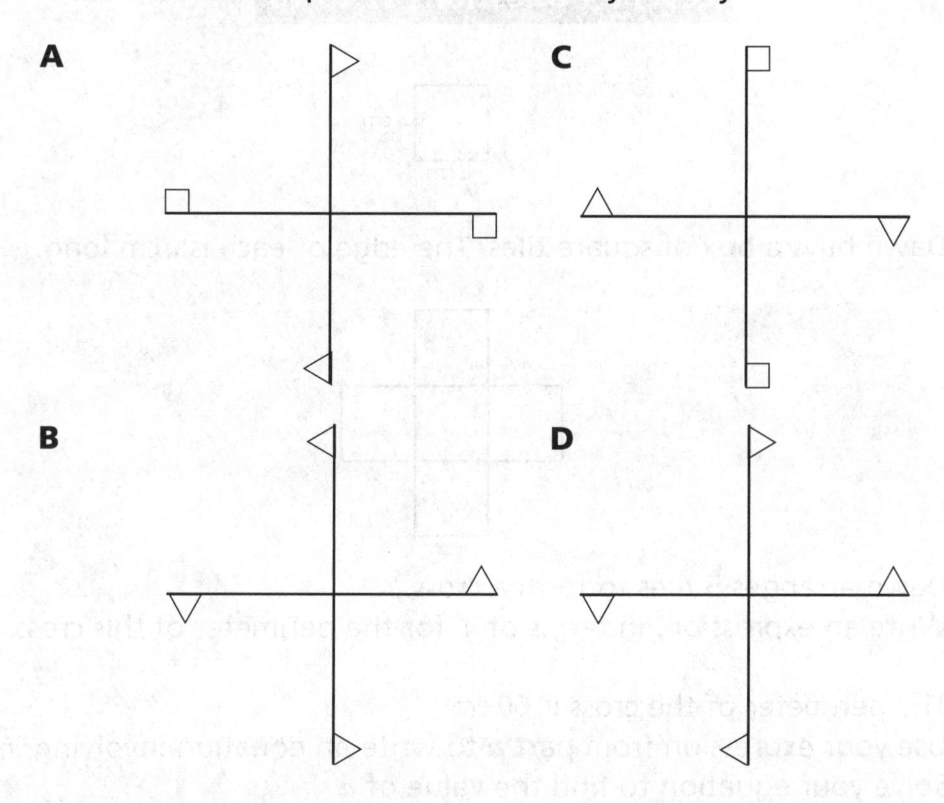

a Which shape does not have rotational symmetry?

b Write down the order of rotational symmetry for each of the other three shapes.

c Which shape has line symmetry and rotational symmetry? Copy it and draw any axis of symmetry using a broken line.

d In how many different ways can you make one small change to the shape that does not have rotational symmetry so that it has rotational symmetry?
Illustrate each change with a sketch.

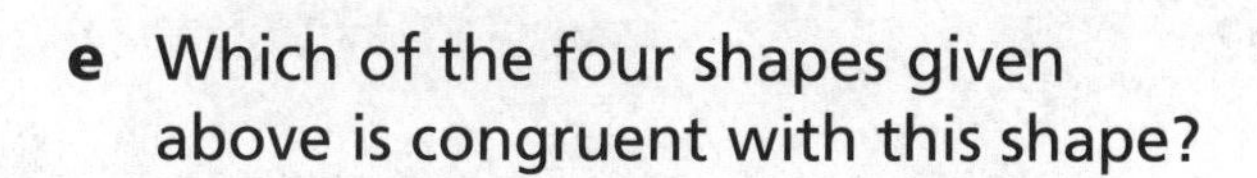

e Which of the four shapes given above is congruent with this shape?

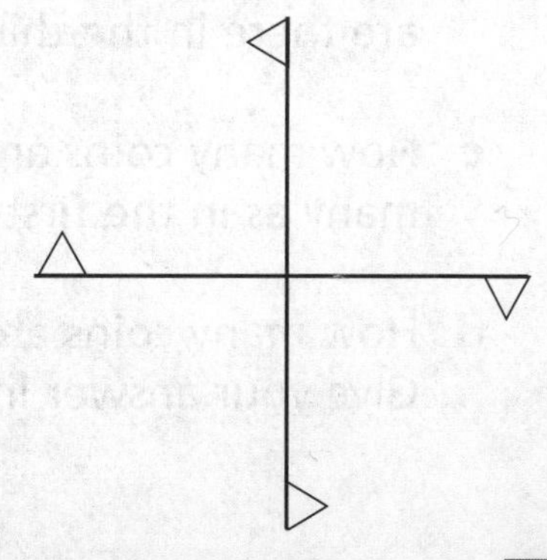

12.

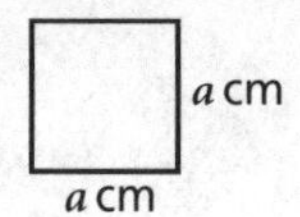

Dawn buys a box of square tiles. The edge of each is a cm long.

a

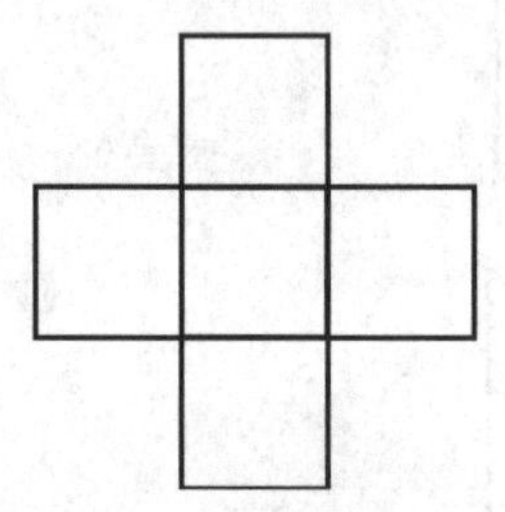

Dawn arranges 5 tiles to form a cross.
Write an expression, in terms of a, for the perimeter of this cross.

b The perimeter of the cross is 60 cm.
Use your expression from part **a** to write an equation involving a.
Solve your equation to find the value of a.

13. Doug has 4 piles of coins.
The first pile has n coins in it.

a How many coins are there in the second pile if there are 5 more than in the first pile?

b The third pile has 2 fewer coins than the first pile. How many coins are there in the third pile?

c How many coins are there in the fourth pile if there are 3 times as many as in the first pile?

d How many coins are there altogether?
Give your answer in its simplest form.

14.

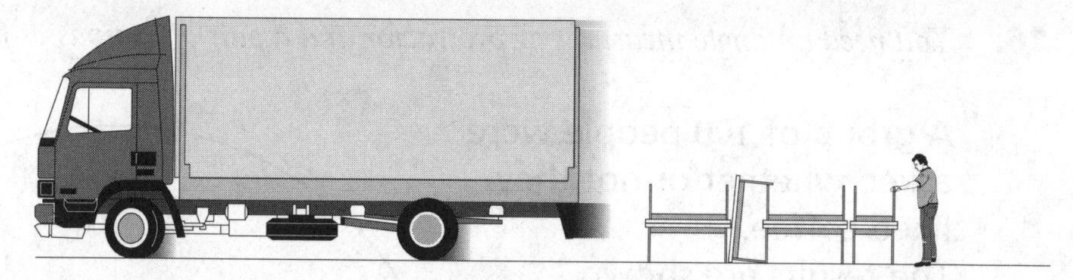

A new school has 26 classrooms. Each classroom needs 29 desks.

a How many desks are needed altogether?

b The first delivery of furniture for the school includes 500 desks. How many classrooms can be given a full set of desks?

c When the second delivery of furniture arrives the lorry is carrying 250 desks. Are there now enough desks? Explain your answer.

15a

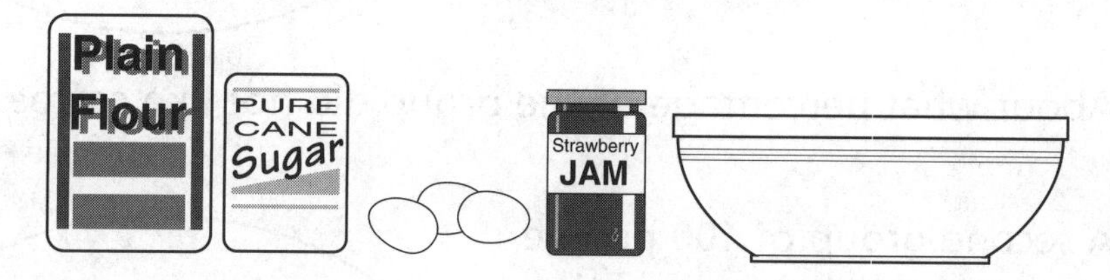

The ingredients for a sponge cake in an old recipe book that Kate is given are

> 4 oz plain flour, $4\frac{1}{2}$ oz castor sugar, 3 eggs,
> grated lemon, pinch of salt, jam

Convert the weights of the ingredients into metric measurements (100 g ≈ 3.5 oz).

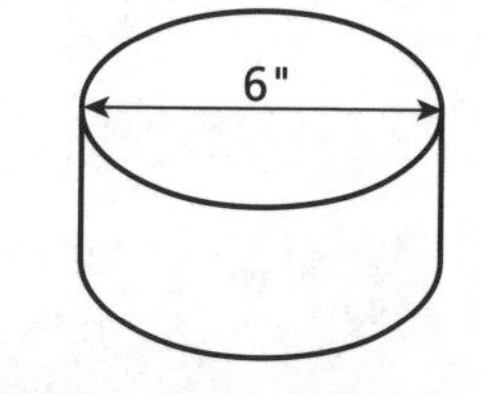

The mixture is then placed in a circular 6 inch tin and baked at 338°F.

b Find, in centimetres, the approximate diameter of the tin.

c To change degrees Fahrenheit (°F) into degrees Celsius (°C) Kate uses the formula

$$C = \frac{5}{9}(F - 32)$$

Use this formula to find the temperature in degrees Celsius at which the oven should be set to bake the sponge.

16. *You need an angle measurer or protractor and a pair of compasses for this question.*

A group of 100 people were asked whether or not they liked coffee.
The results are shown in the pie chart.

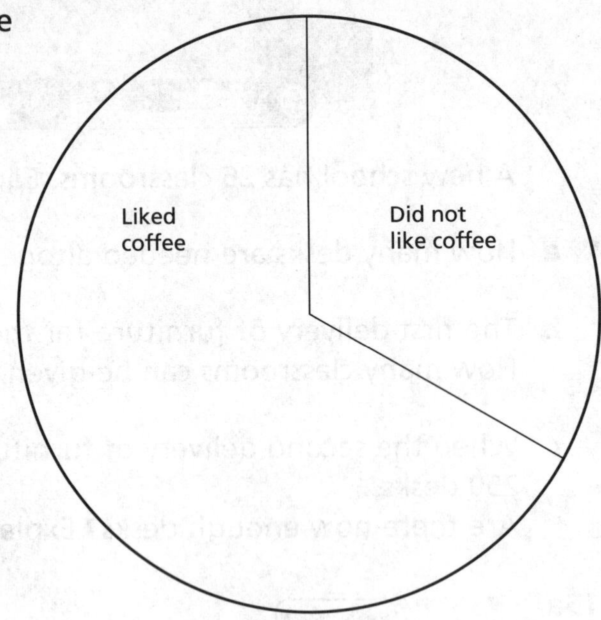

a About what percentage of the group did not like coffee?

A second group of 100 people were asked the same question.
The results are shown in the second pie chart.

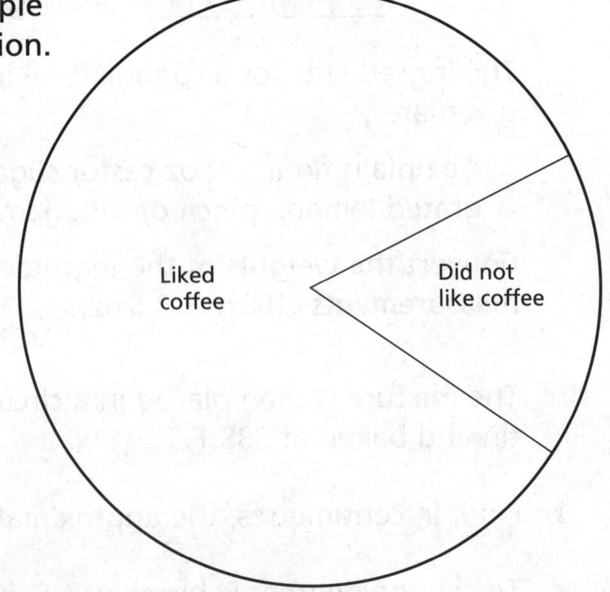

b About what percentage of this group like coffee?

c The information from the two groups is combined.
Draw a pie chart to show how the total of 200 people liked or disliked coffee.

Level 6 • Questions 17 to 21

17a Rory draws a square that has a perimeter of 40 cm. What is the area of this square?

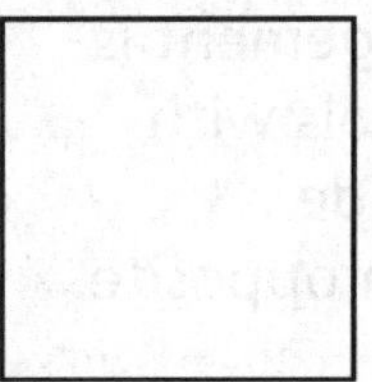

b

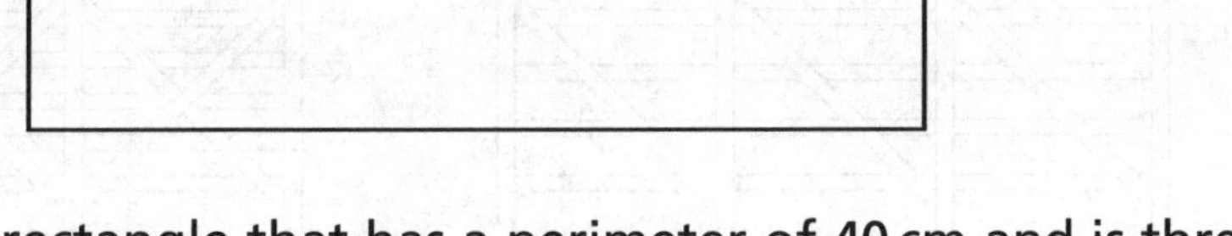

Stuart draws a rectangle that has a perimeter of 40 cm and is three times as long as it is wide.
What is the area of the rectangle?

18. Rabbit pâté is sold in tins like this:

a The area of the base of each tin is 24 cm^2 and each tin is 3 cm deep.
What volume of pâté is in one tin?

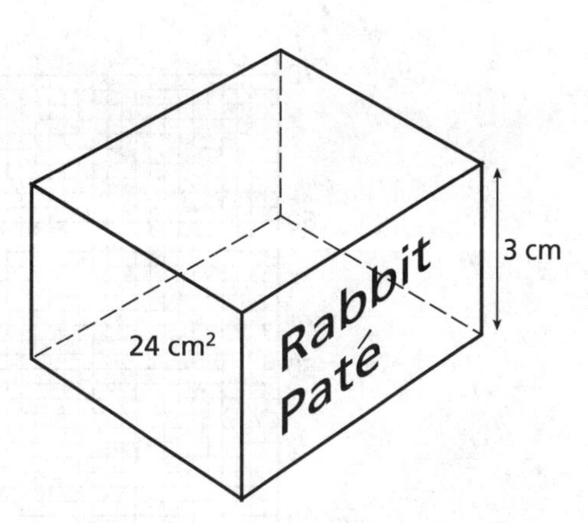

b

The label goes around the tin and overlaps by 1 cm.
If the area of the label is 63.6 cm^2 work out the distance around the edge of the tin.

c New cylindrical tins are to be introduced. They will be 5.5 cm in diameter and 3.5 cm deep. What volume of pâté will the new tin hold?

19. Will is investigating the number of lengths of timber needed to make sections for fencing sheep.

The simplest arrangement is to have 3 horizontals with verticals on each side arranged as shown opposite.

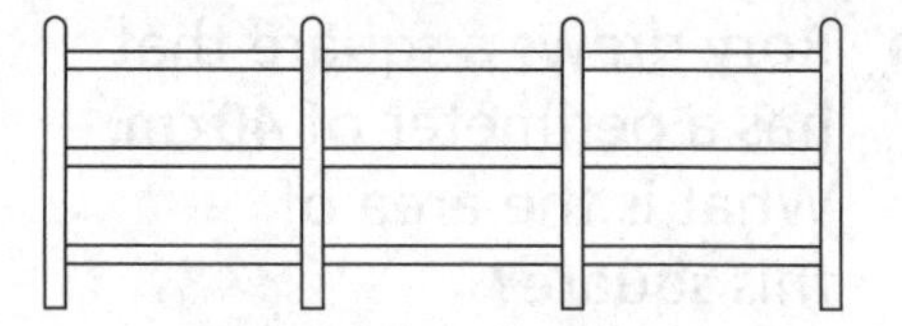

Next he tried 4 horizontals with a diagonal bar i.e.

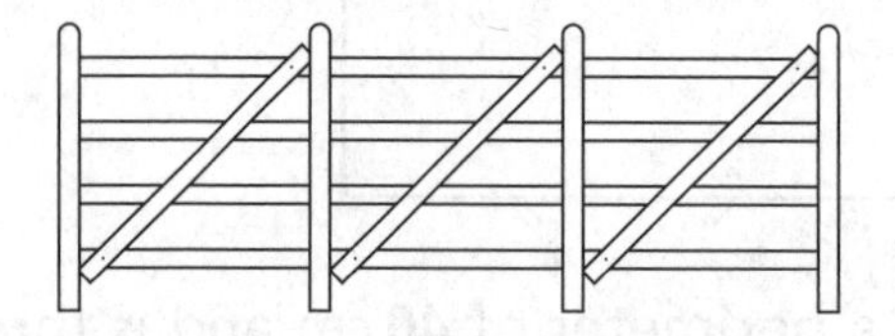

and finally 5 horizontals with 2 diagonal bars i.e

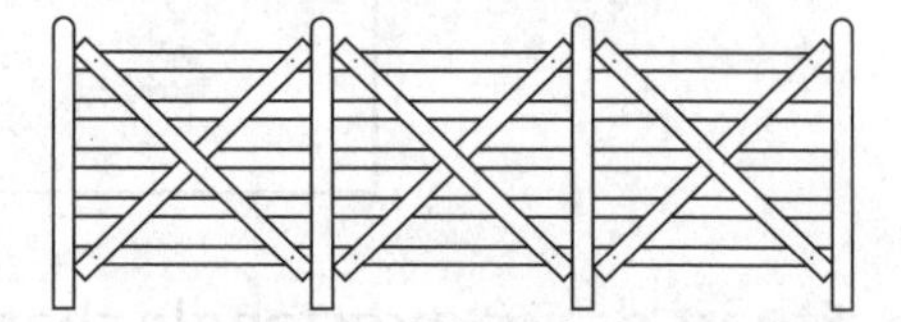

Will drew graphs to show how the total number of lengths needed was related to the number of sections.

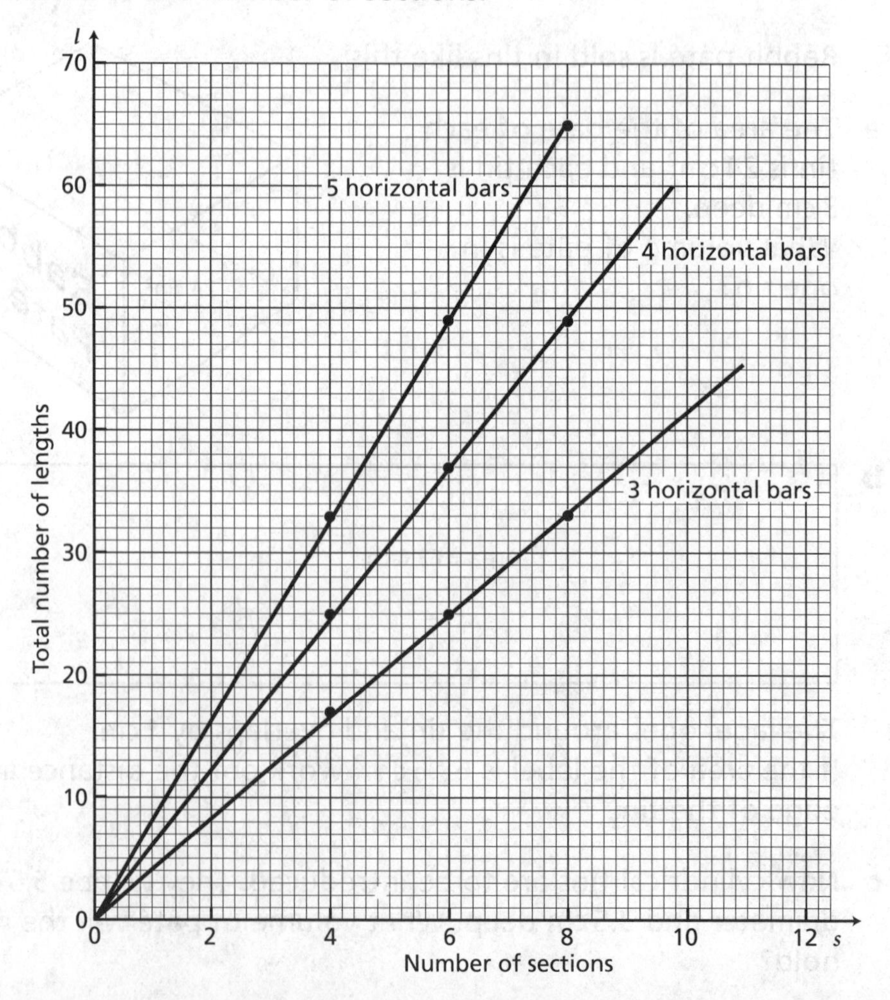

The equation for the number l of lengths needed to make s sections when each section has 3 horizontal bars between the posts is $l = 4s + 1$.

When there are 4 horizontal bars in each section the formula is $l = 6s + 1$ and when there are 5 horizontal bars in each section the formula is $l = 8s + 1$.

Will has 41 lengths of timber.

a Use the correct graph to find the number of sections that can be made when there are **5** horizontal bars in each section.

b How many sections can be made if there are 4 horizontal lengths in each section?

c The straight line through the points for the equation $l = 8s + 1$ is steeper than the line through the points for the equation $l = 6s + 1$ and the line through the points for the equation $l = 4s + 1$.

Which part of the equation $l = 8s + 1$ tells us how steep the line is?

d Plot 3 points to show the graph when there are 2 horizontal bars and no diagonal.

What is the equation of the straight line passing through these 3 points?

20.

Year	United Kingdom	England	Wales	Scotland	N. Ireland
1981	56 354	46 821	2814		1539
1991	57 801	48 208	2891	5107	1594
2001		49 921	2961	5148	1686
2011	61 110	51 289	3010		1733

The table shows the populations in **thousands**, including the probable figures for the year 2001 and the year 2011, for the various parts of the United Kingdom at 10-year intervals.

a Use the table to work out the population of Scotland in 1981.

b Work out the expected population of the United Kingdom in the year 2001.

c In 1991 what percentage of the population of the United Kingdom lived in England? Give your answer correct to the nearest whole number.

d In 1981, for every person who lived in Northern Ireland how many lived in England?

e Tony said that the population of every region in the UK is expected to show an increase from 1991 to 2001. Explain why Tony is correct.

f Ben looked at the projected figures for 2011. He reasoned that since the four given figures were larger than the corresponding figure for 2001 the figure for Scotland in 2011 must also be bigger than the figure for Scotland in 2001.
Explain why you think Ben's reasoning is sound or why you think it is flawed.

g Use the table to work out the projected population of Scotland in 2011. Was Ben correct?

21. Eight Year 9 pupils decided to find out whether there was any relationship between their heights, weights, the amount of time they spent doing homework and the amount of time they spent watching television. They collected data for one week and plotted the three scatter graphs given below.

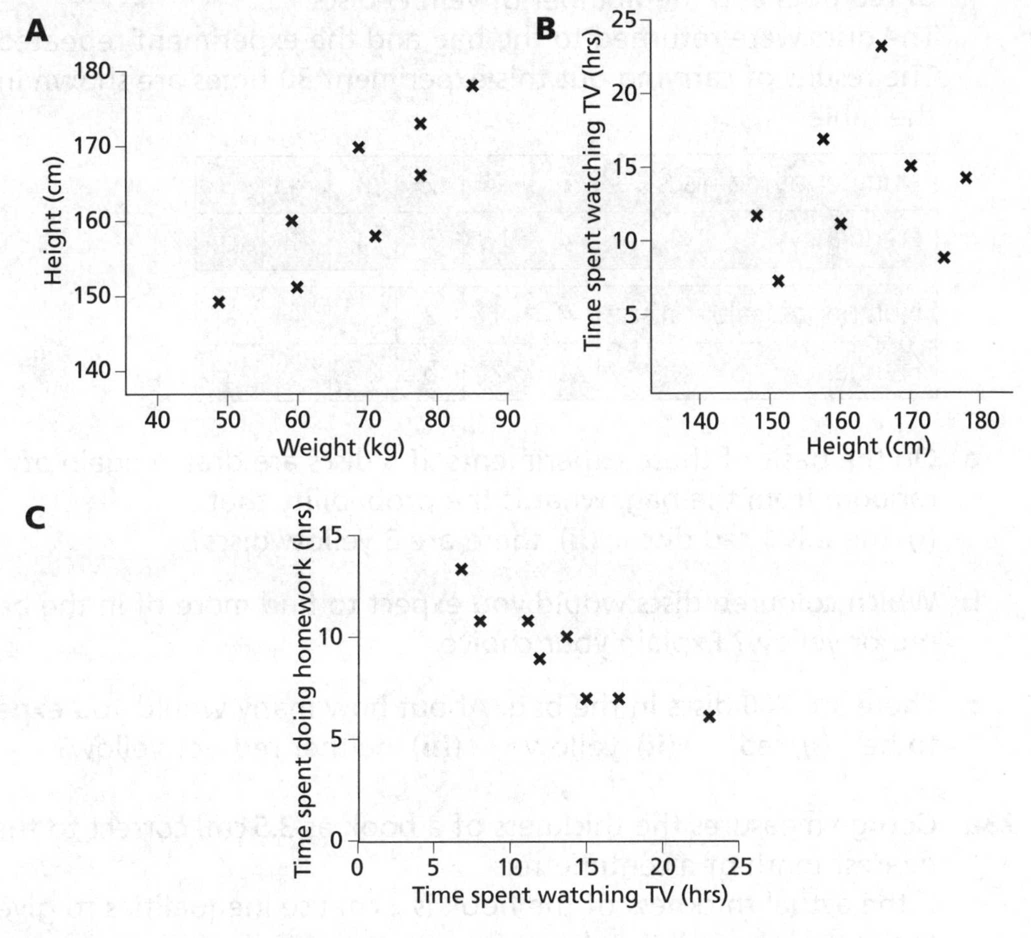

a What does graph **A** tell us about the relationship between the height and weight of these eight pupils?

b What does graph **B** tell us about the relationship between a pupils' height and the number of hours that pupil spent watching television?

c What does graph **C** tell us about the relationship between the number of hours a pupil spent doing homework and the number of hours that pupil spent watching television?

d Santo joined the group. He said that he weighed 64 kg and that he spent 12 hours doing homework last week. What other information about Santo could you infer using these graphs?

22. Gordon has a bag of coloured discs.
He took 5 discs at random out of the bag and counted the number of red discs and the number of yellow discs.
The discs were returned to the bag and the experiment repeated.
The results of carrying out this experiment 30 times are shown in the table.

Number of red discs	0	1	2	3	4	5
Frequency	4	16	5	4	1	0

Number of yellow discs	0	1	2	3	4	5
Frequency	0	2	5	17	5	1

a On the basis of these experiments, if 5 discs are drawn again at random from the bag, what is the probability that
(i) there is 1 red disc **(ii)** there are 3 yellow discs?

b Which coloured discs would you expect to find more of in the bag: red or yellow? Explain your choice.

c There are 200 discs in the bag. About how many would you expect to be **(i)** red **(ii)** yellow **(iii)** neither red nor yellow?

23a George measures the thickness of a book as 3.5 cm, correct to the nearest tenth of a centimetre.
If the actual thickness of the book is x cm use inequalities to give the range of possible values of x.

b Sue's height is given as 1.74 m. Is this figure correct to the nearest tenth of a metre or to the nearest centimetre?
What, in millimetres, is her smallest possible height?

c Andy wants to buy a display cabinet to fit in an alcove in his lounge. He measures the width of the alcove and finds it is 81 cm, correct to the nearest centimetre. In the furniture store the salesman assures Andy that the cabinet he chooses is also 81 cm wide, correct to the nearest centimetre, but when it is delivered and Andy tries to fit it into the alcove it is too wide. Explain how this is possible even though both Andy and the salesman have measured correctly.

24.

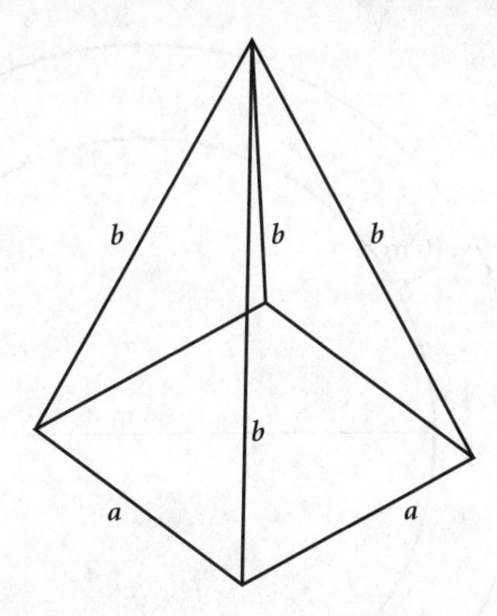

To work out the surface area (A) and volume (V) of this square pyramid Jo uses the formulas

$$A = a^2 + 2a \times \sqrt{b^2 - \frac{a^2}{4}}$$

$$V = \tfrac{1}{3}a^2 \times \sqrt{b^2 - \frac{a^2}{2}}$$

a The edges of the base of a square pyramid are 3.5 cm and the length of each slant height is 4.6 cm.

Find the value of $3.5^2 + 2 \times 3.5 \times \sqrt{4.6^2 - \frac{3.5^2}{4}}$

What is the surface area of the pyramid?
Give your answer in cm^2.

b Find the volume of the pyramid in cm^3.

25a The table shows values of x and y for the equation $y = x^2 + 2x - 7$.
Copy and complete the table.

x	−3	−2	−1	0	1	2	3
y				−7	−4	1	

b The value of x that gives $y = 0$ is between 1 and 2.
Find, by trial and improvement and correct to 1 decimal place, the value of x that gives y closest to 0.

26.

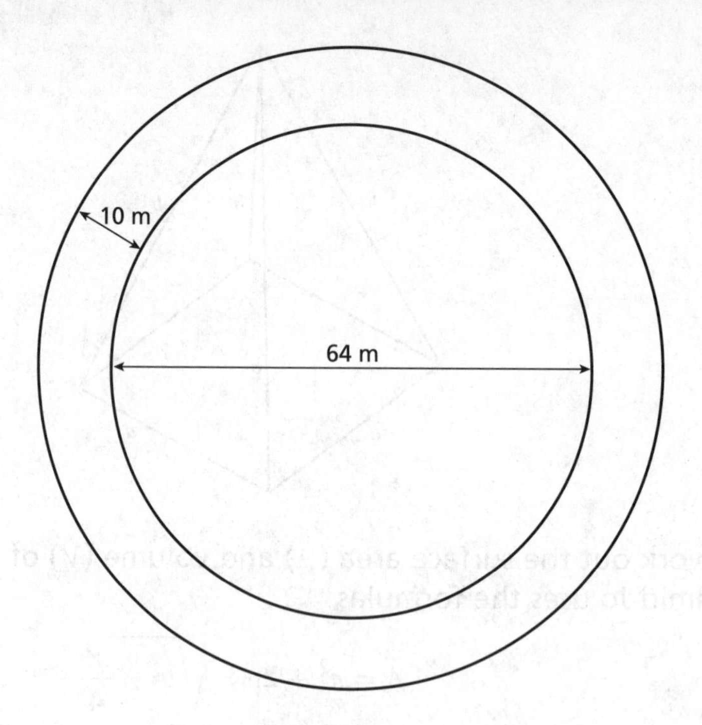

A running track 10 m wide surrounds a circular sports' field of diameter 64 m.

a Find the area of the sports' field.

b Find the combined area of the track and the field.

c Hence find the area of the running track.

d

How much further than Tim does Ken run if Ken runs one circuit on the outside of the track and Tim runs one circuit on the inside of the track?

Give all your answers correct to 3 significant figures.

Level 8 • Questions 27 to 30

27. Last year there were 200 pupils in Year 9 at Eastwood School. At the end of the Christmas term every pupil took a test in English and in maths. The maximum mark on each test was 50. The results are shown in the graph.

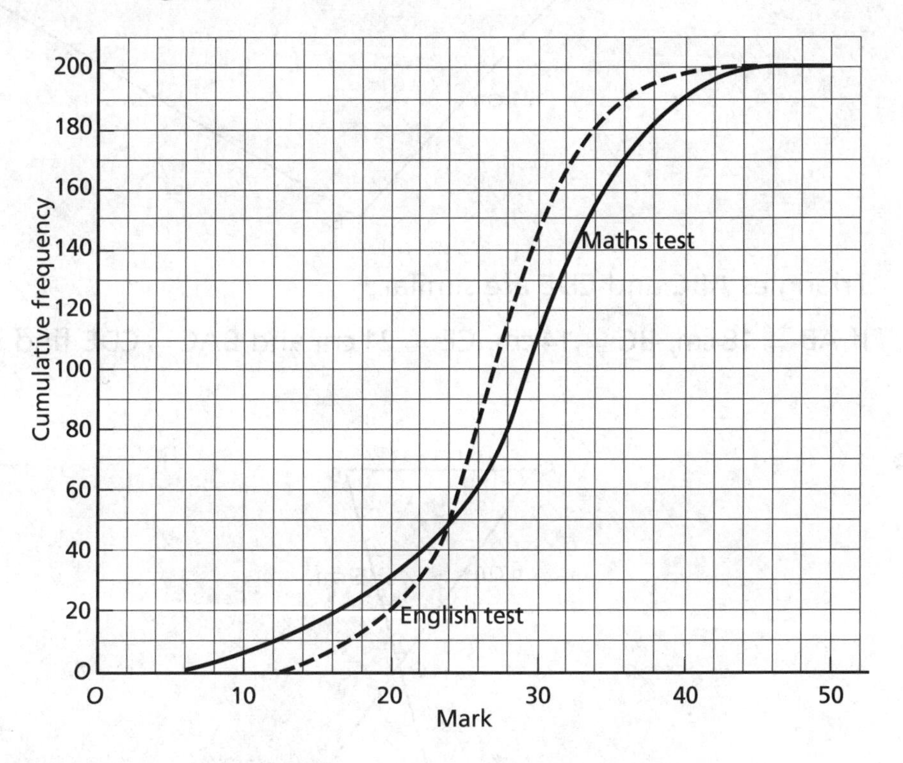

a What was the lowest mark in **(i)** maths **(ii)** English?

b What was the highest mark in **(i)** maths **(ii)** English?

c What mark was scored by the same number of pupils in maths and in English?

d Daniel said that the median mark in English was 27 and that the median mark in maths was just below 30. Was Daniel correct? Explain your answer.

e Is it true to say that most pupils scored a higher mark in English than in maths?

f What was the lowest mark in maths scored by a pupil in the top 20%?

g What was the highest mark in English scored by a pupil in the bottom 20%?

28a

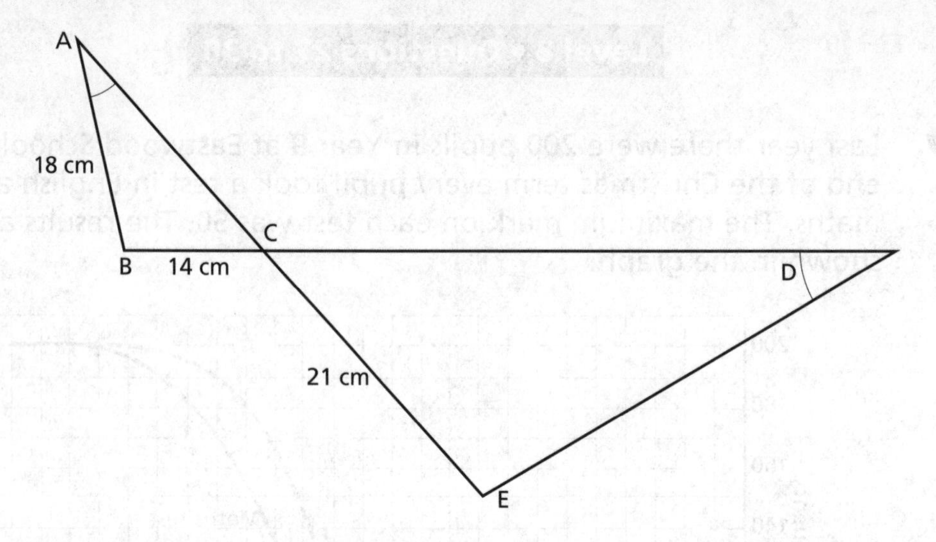

Triangles ABC and CDE are similar.

If AB = 18 cm, BC = 14 cm, CE = 21 cm and $B\hat{A}C = C\hat{D}E$ find DE.

b

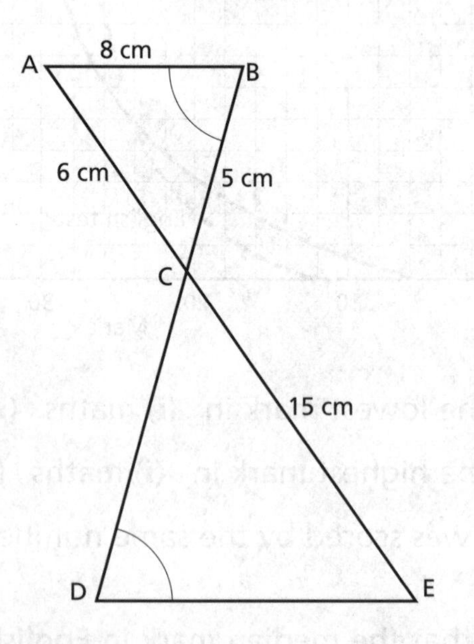

Triangles ABC and EDC are similar.

AB = 8 cm, AC = 6 cm, BC = 5 cm, CE = 15 cm and $A\hat{B}C = C\hat{D}E$.
Calculate the length of **(i)** DE **(ii)** DC.
Show your working.

29. A sphere of radius r is cut by two parallel planes, whose distances from the centre of the sphere are a and $a+h$, to give a slice of the sphere. The volume, V, of the slice is given by the formula

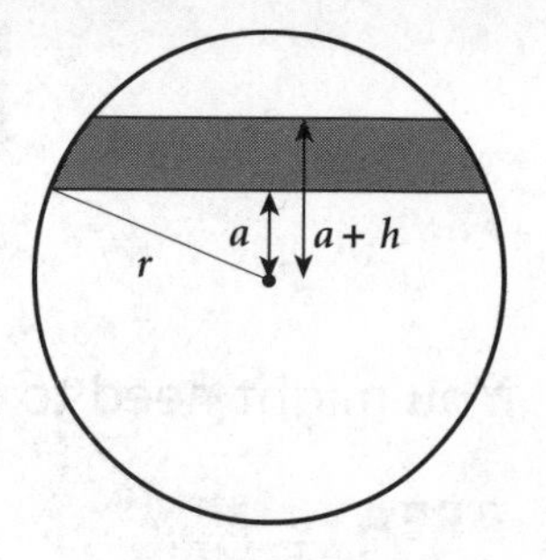

$$V = \pi h(r^2 - a^2 - ah - \tfrac{1}{3}h^2)$$

a Find the volume of the slice when $r = 5.6\,\text{cm}$, $a = 2.4\,\text{cm}$ and $h = 1.8\,\text{cm}$.

b The surface area of the slice, A, is given by the formula

$$A = 2\pi\left(r^2 + rh - a^2 - ah - \frac{h^2}{2}\right)$$

Use this formula to find the surface area of the slice referred to in part **a**.

30. For each equation, give the number of the curve it could represent.

a $y = -x^2$

b $y = \dfrac{10}{x}$

c $y = -3x$

d $y = x^3$

e $y = x^2 - 6$

f $y = x^2(1 - x)$

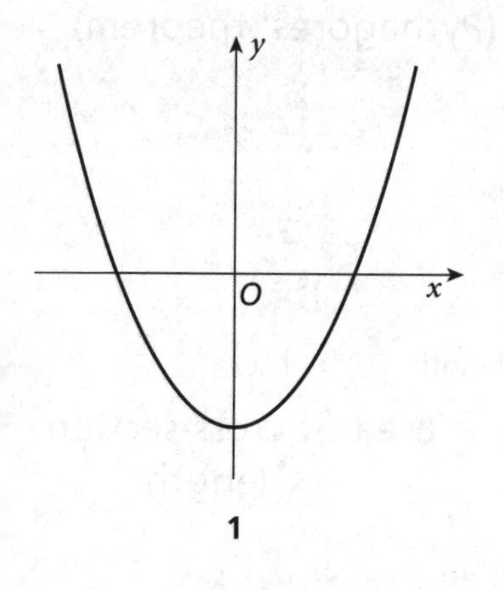

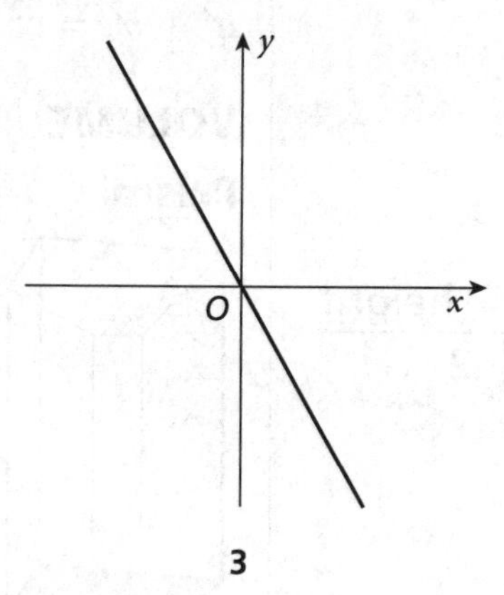

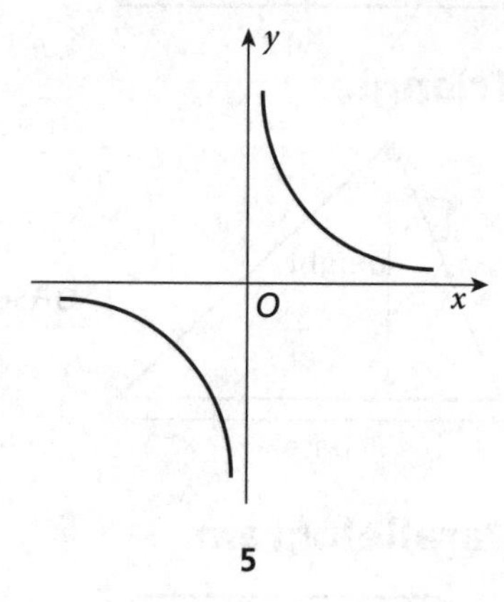

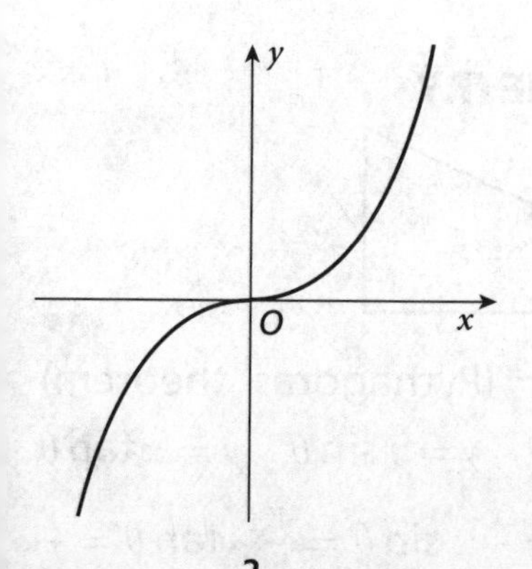

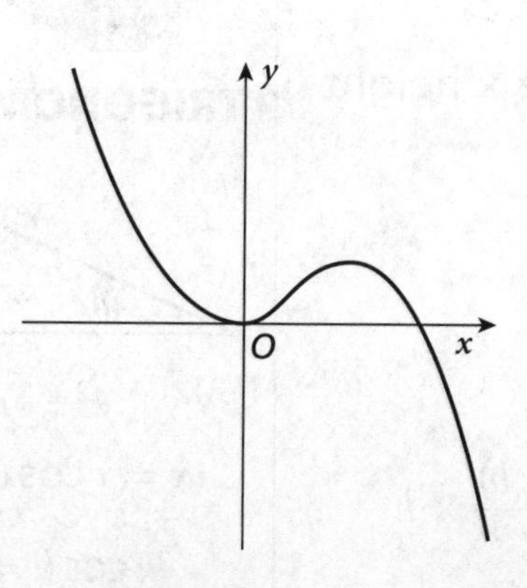

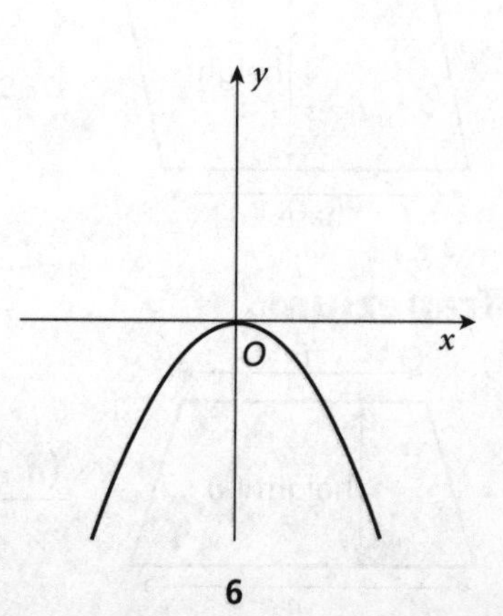

FORMULAE

You might need to use these formulae.

AREA

Circle

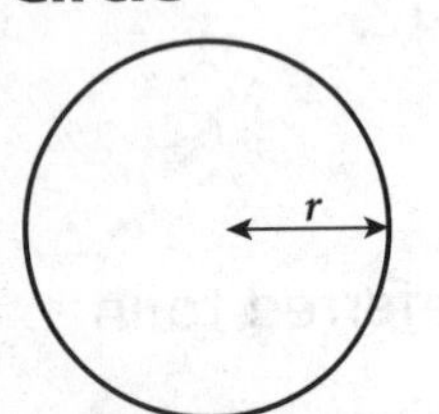

πr^2

Rectangle

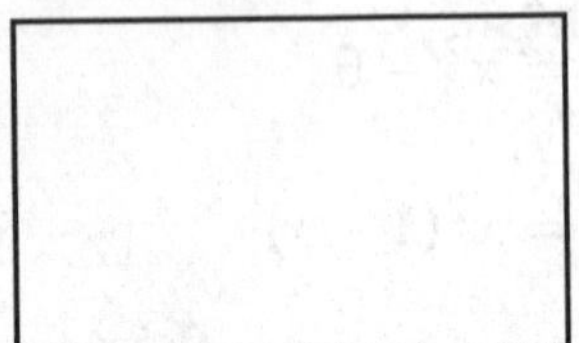

length × width

Triangle

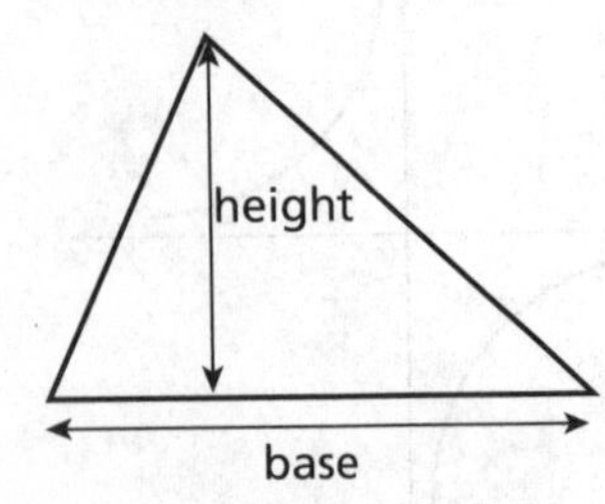

$\frac{\text{base} \times \text{height}}{2}$

Parallelogram

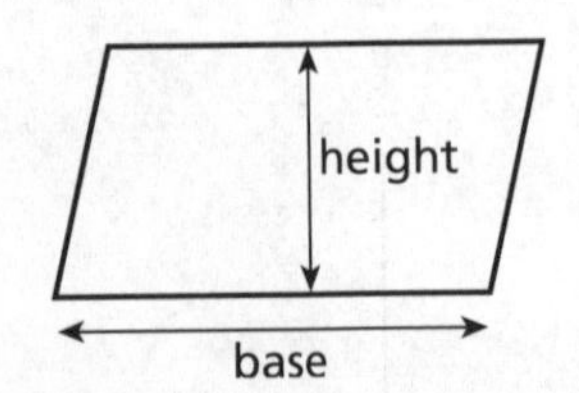

base × height

Trapezium

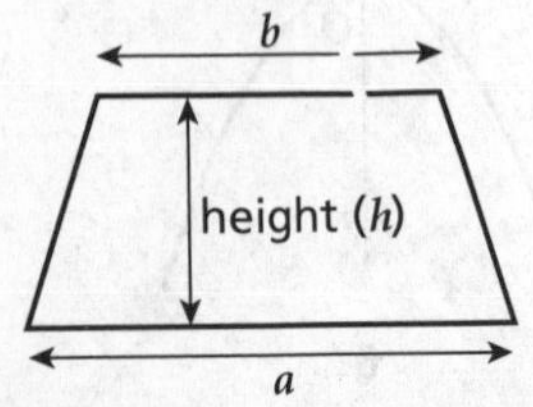

$\frac{(a+b)}{2} \times h$

LENGTH

Circle

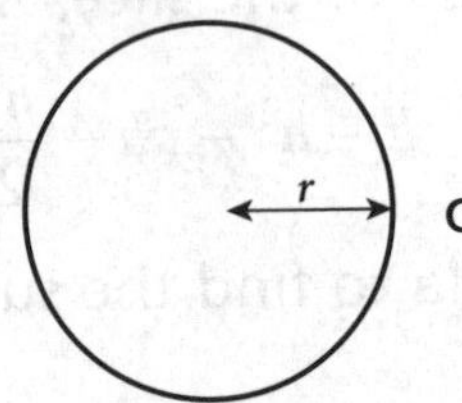

circumference $= 2\pi r$

For a right-angled triangle

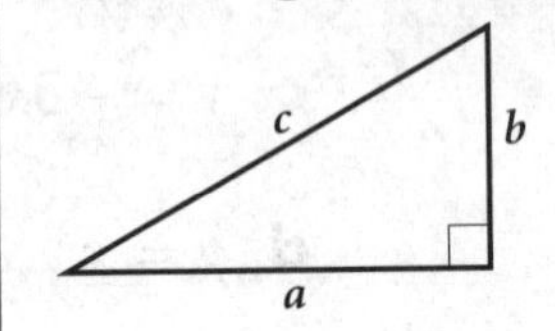

$a^2 + b^2 = c^2$ (Pythagoras' theorem)

VOLUME

Prism

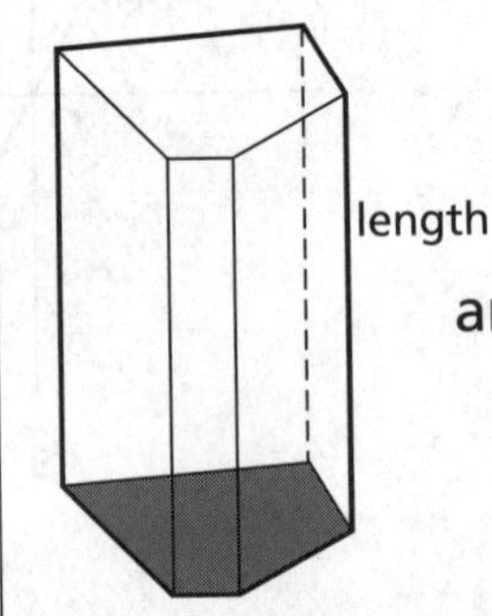

area of cross-section × length

TRIGONOMETRY

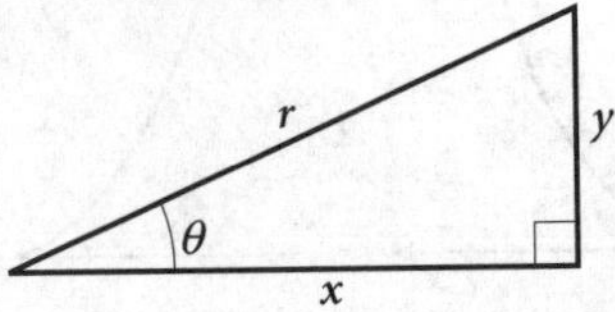

$x^2 + y^2 = r^2$ (Pythagoras' theorem)

$x = r\cos\theta \quad y = r\sin\theta \quad y = x\tan\theta$

$\cos\theta = \frac{x}{r} \quad \sin\theta = \frac{y}{r} \quad \tan\theta = \frac{y}{x}$